Your invitation said "No Gifts Please"

So ◁ **W9-AHE-230**

This book is on
Permanent and Perpetual
Loan

To Elder and Mrs. H. T. Terry

With our compliments and
best wishes —

Florence & Adlai Esteb

See pages 120 and 121
for Growing Old Gracefully
and Stay Young

Rosewood

AND OTHER POEMS

By

Adlai Albert Esteb, B.Th., M.A., Ph.D.

Author of DRIFTWOOD, FIREWOOD, SANDALWOOD,
MORNING MANNA

REVIEW AND HERALD PUBLISHING ASSOCIATION
WASHINGTON, D.C.

IN TRIBUTE TO THE AUTHOR

"We hear you loud and clear." This reassurance from the ground forces at Canaveral, now Cape Kennedy, heartened our pioneer astronauts in their orbital flights through the stratosphere. Poets who capture life's ideals and the unspoken aspirations of the human heart in lilting lines that need no interpreter find a similar response in an admiring and grateful public.

The facile verse of Dr. Esteb in his previously published volumes, *Driftwood, Firewood,* and *Sandalwood,* has established his popularity with a wide reader audience as a master of metrical moods that move the heart. As laureate of lively lyrics that stir the soul, his reputation is secure. This fourth collection of verse, *Rosewood,* as did his other anthologies, comprises poems written out of rich experience and broad contacts with peoples of varied race and nationality. They ring with the assurances of Christian faith and confidence in the divine destiny proclaimed in the gospel for men and women who accept God's provision of grace for every believer.

The narrative theme poem "Rosewood" establishes the reader's rapport with the author's reminiscent and creative moods in successive sections of the book. The zest of romance is added in many of the poems by indicating in a footnote the place and sometimes the hour of composition, for they are spiced with references to the exotic corners of the earth which evoked the muse on the writer's many travels. The Christian graces of good cheer, tolerance, gentility, sympathy, and perspicacious humor permeate the verse throughout, so that immediacy of meaning is one of its special charms. Many a speaker finds quotable lines here and there to adorn or accent his public messages. We have no hesitancy in proclaiming this to be a volume to be treasured as comparable with Dr. Esteb's previously published works, if not superior to them in scope and coverage of topics. —H. M. TIPPETT

In Praise of Poetry

Poetry is the exquisite expression of exquisite impressions.—
J. BOUX.

Pure poetry paints rainbows in our tears—
Distills life's sweetest nectar from the years;
How many precious lessons it imparts,
While pulling thorns from bruised and bleeding hearts.
It gathers perfume from the blushing rose,
And blessings finds in wildest wind that blows;
It rides the fiery chariots of the skies,
And kindles faith to flash from smiling eyes.

It tunes our hearts to whispers from above,
And helps us hear the answering chords of love;
A moment's insight brings to our dull sense,
As much as lifetime study might dispense.
It builds a magic bridge to worlds afar,
And reads the secrets of each shining star.
It whispers peace in all our mortal strife,
And holds the key to more abundant life.

It sweetens sorrow with a touch divine,
Extracts from piercing pain life's purest wine.
It shows the values in our direst loss,
Reveals perpetual glory in Christ's cross.
It elevates man's culture and his arts,
And strikes the highest note within our hearts,
Inspiring us to sing, as on we plod,
Life's sweetest music man can render God.

Pure poetry is man's eternal friend,
And brings to life its richest dividend.

CONTENTS

I. AT DAWN WITH GOD

II. AT WORK WITH GOD

III. OVER PARAPETS OF THE WORLD

IV. ASPIRATION

V. IN MERRIER MOOD

Rosewood

I gathered DRIFTWOOD many years
From Eastern, Western hemispheres.
It made the fairest FIREWOOD too,
With pyrotechnical review;
Their tongues of fire told me, indeed,
Why some men fail and some succeed.
'Twas thus that SANDALWOOD became
A new book o'er the writer's name.
At last ROSEWOOD has come along,
With new notes in the poet's song.

While wand'ring on an ancient trail,
I stumbled on my latest tale,
For there I found a rare antique
Half buried near a mountain creek.
It was a vase that caught my eye;
It was about twelve inches high.
Immersed in mud, it was a sight,
Until a scrubbing made it bright.
It was, indeed, a work of art
That must have come from someone's heart.
And hidden there within the vase
Were golden locks and dainty lace.
Beneath rose petals buried deep
Was something someone tried to keep.

It was an ancient rusty key.
Was it the key to mystery?
Well, here was where the tale began,
A tale to stir the mind of man.

Why was this rose vase buried here?
And was the key to something near?
Intrigued, I thought I'd look around
To see if treasure might be found.

Nearby I found a mountain spring;
It didn't seem to mean a thing
Until I spied an ancient trail
Beside a rustic fence of rail.
It led me to a plot of ground
With ruins lying all around.
Was this the home of pioneers
Who suffered much through tragic years?
They must have fled; I never knew;
I saw an arrowhead or two.

I found a box; I had the key.
Alas, it was no use to me,
For those who robbed had smashed the chest,
Grabbed what they wanted, left the rest.
They took what treasure they could find,
But left the greatest gem behind—
They left a mother's diary,
And what a prize it proved to be!
For what I read in faded ink
Soon forged a story, link by link—
A saga writ with blood and tears,
The legend of our pioneers!

They started life in Delaware;
They built their first log cabin there.
A little baby came along,
Then came the ev'ning cradle song.
She held her cherub on her lap
And sang for her to take a nap.
Then came the Indians with alarms
And snatched their darling from their arms.
There followed several empty years—
A test for even pioneers!

When peace had come and wars had ceased,
Then all white children were released.
The Indian chief without much noise,
Had gathered all white girls and boys,
And they were herded to a line
And faced white mothers at a sign.
The children stood there, filled with fear,
Each trembling like a frightened deer.
They only spoke the Indian tongue,
For they were kidnaped very young.
Though strange, unkempt, and very wild,
Yet each was still his mother's child.
All in a row each faced a mother,
Yet neither recognized the other.
Not even one child knew his name;
Yet mother love was just the same.
For years each one had offered prayer,
And now at last her child was there.
But what a grievous gulf between!
No language could describe the scene,
And no one knew just what to do,
For not a single mother knew

Her own dear child from all the rest—
What agony in ev'ry breast!

This precious diary did unfold
The anguish that could not be told.
She lifted up her heart in prayer
For help to find her darling there.
Then suddenly, so sweet and low,
She sang some songs of long ago.
She tried one baby lullaby
(For years it always made her cry)
And then the strangest thing occurred—
One little girl, with one sweet word,
Cried, "Mamma," and with childish charms
She leaped into her mother's arms.

Then other mothers, taking heart,
Began to use this subtle art.
The method worked, to their surprise,
A strange light filled the children's eyes
As dark drapes of the past were drawn,
With light of recognition's dawn.
The dawn indeed of one grand day—
Their children had come home to stay.

In this amazing episode
We see the grace of God bestowed.
The kidnaped prodigals of earth
May seem to be of little worth;
And yet they will respond to love
And songs of Father's home above.
They've wandered far; they've wandered long;
And yet there must be some sweet song

Will strike responsive chords within
And bring them freedom from their sin.
May God prepare our hearts and throats
To sing with softer, sweeter notes,
Till all God's children do respond—
Let's welcome home each vagabond!

The diary told of happy days;
The old log house was full of praise.
Their happiness soon banished tears,
Eclipsed those sad and wasted years.
The parents loved their darling girl,
And watched her toss each golden curl.
But Delaware was crowded now;
They'd like to have more land to plow.
So they began the journey West,
And found this mountain place of rest.
They liked this clear, cool, crystal stream—
They'd make their spot a place to dream.

Then wedding bells rang out one year;
Their girl became a pioneer.
For her brave heart and her bold beau
Had heard the call of "Wesward Ho."
So they began their trek with zest,
To pioneer the golden West.

For hours I pondered what I'd read;
I'd heard the voices of the dead.
I thought of all the toil and tears
That marked the plight of pioneers.
Beside the ruins of that log house
I thanked God for each patient spouse,

The wives of all our pioneers.
They've earned the harvest of the years!
I held with awe this ROSEWOOD vase,
And saw emerging one sweet face,
The face of my own mother dear—
And every other pioneer!

Music Lives On

It's passing strange that when I close my eyes
    To all intruding, transient things around,
Ensuing silence brings a sweet surprise—
    I hear some symphony of half-hushed sound.

The ancient cello I heard yesterday,
    This morn I heard again in vibrant tone.
Can it be true that music lives alway,
    And starts pulsating sound-waves all its own?

Can I be sure that ev'ry note I strike
    Lives on and on and never has to die?
Just like the words I speak into a mike
    Will orbit earth in twinkling of an eye?

This probing thought should stab us all awake;
    It is a matter no one dares ignore.
Will all we do or say, with each mistake—
    The music of our lives—be heard once more?

SECTION 1

At Dawn With God

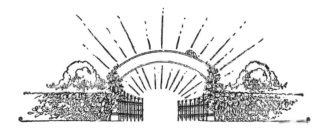

At Dawn With God

I daily seek for wisdom, grace, and power
To live for Christ and walk with Him each hour;
I come each morn with hungry heart and mind,
To learn the holy art of being kind;
I pray for clearer vision as my eyes
Pierce dawn's east window of divine surprise!

Doorway of the Day

The doorway of the morning opens wide,
Inviting us to come and step inside
And gather treasures of the day just born,
The riches and the freshness of the morn;
And while the diamonds sparkle in the dew,
Consider what this day could hold for you.

Before you pass the portals of this day,
Accept the opportunity to pray,
And, as the camel kneels to take his load
Before he starts along his dusty road,
So make the preparation for your way
While kneeling at the doorway of the day.

Reveille at Dawn

What makes the flowers lift up their heads,
    To greet the rising sun?
All nature feels the pull of power,
    When new day has begun.
Why do the birds begin to stir,
    And sing their songs of cheer?
Are their ears tuned to new wave lengths
    Which our dull ears can't hear?
Is there a reveille at dawn
    Which makes the birds rejoice?
It comes at sunrise ev'ry day—
    Why can't we hear God's voice?

Sunrise

The mind of man requires some silent time,
  For sacred themes;
We need a quiet, holy place sublime,
  For nobler dreams.
This noisy world in which we live each hour,
  Each busy day,
Disintegrates our poise, our peace, our power—
  We need to pray!

Where can we find that quiet time and place?
  Where shall we go
Where we may gaze upon our Master's face,
  And soul can grow?
There is no noise at daybreak; turn your eyes
  While dawn is still,
And gaze upon the beauty of the skies
  And dew-kissed hill.

For in the hush of quiet dawn, what power!
  Unmeasured sums*
Of energy are loosed on earth the hour
  When sunrise comes!

---

*It is reported that in three minutes time more energy from the sun, in the form of *light* and *heat*, comes to our earth than from all the coal consumed in all the world in a whole year.

Not by Bread Alone

We cannot live by bread alone,
For man is more than flesh and bone.

We live by beauty—flowers that please the eyes;
The glory and the peace of tranquil skies;
By fleecy clouds when etched with silver light,
By twinkling stars that scintillate all night.

We cannot live by bread alone,
Or by the gains our books have shown.
Instead, by harmonies that charm our ears,
Like whispering pines, dissolve our haunting fears;
By songbird singing songs that so enthrall,
Or majesty of some great waterfall.

We cannot live by bread alone,
Or by the things we call our own.
We live by faith, by hope, by peace and rest
When sunset's glory paints the golden west.
Our sweetest moments come at eventide
When, meeting God, our souls are satisfied!

The Hour of Power

Oh, what painter's brush
Made the crimson blush
Mid the silent hush
  Of this fresh new day?

In this radiant dawn,
With the darkness gone,
While the Lord looks on—
  What a time to pray!

For this quiet hour
Is the one of power;
Ev'ry dew-kissed flower
  Feels the heav'nly shower.

So I lift my head
As I leave my bed,
And my hands I spread—
  'Tis my hour of power!

The Hour of Prayer

How precious to come in dawn's early hours,
While gems are still sparkling on dew-kissed flowers,
To pause on the trail of the day to be trod,
And wait in the holy presence of God.

At night the stars shine in the sky supreme;
At dawn in the grass the emeralds gleam;
All nature awakes with the sun's bright rays;
The birds join and sing in a chorus of praise.

How we should rejoice to be made aware
That the time has come for the hour of prayer.
It truly is worship when one will wait
At dawn in the presence of One so great.

Thus we catch visions of God above,
A God of wisdom and power and love.
And we go to our work empowered anew
For whatever the task we are called to do.

What Is Worship?

Worship is *not* merely singing sweet songs
  Or saying prayers or quoting creeds.
Worship requires the forsaking of wrongs,
  And feeling our spiritual needs.

Worship is transacting business with God
  In order to make life complete.
Worship is leaving sin's paths we have trod
  And kneeling at God's mercy seat.

Worship exchanges our needs for God's grace,
  Replaces our weakness with power.
Worship is man gazing up at God's face,
  And getting new strength for each hour.

Worship is hunger—heart hunger for God,
  A craving in man from his youth;
Worship inspires weary people who plod,
  And satisfies thirstings for truth.

Worship is purest communion with God;
  Man pours forth the love of his heart;
Worship is taking God's staff or His rod,
  And all He sees best to impart.

Worship is lifting up tear-stained eyes,
  As a child looks up to be kissed;
Worship finds fellowship, love's great surprise,
  And blessings which most men have missed.

Worship lifts man to new levels of life
　　When worship has come from the heart.
Worship brings triumph in man's mortal strife.
　　Is worship, then, man's highest art?

Worship exalts man above beasts and birds,
　　And leads where earth's greatest have trod.
So don't rate a man by his wealth or his words,
　　But by how he worships his God.

The Power of Worship

The greatest thing about the act of worship is its power
To make us erring mortals diff'rent, from that very hour.
For God forgives the prodigal; gives kisses for his shame;
And one who truly worships God can never be the same.

Which Song Do You Sing?

One day I sang a song of tears,
　　And folks who listened wept;
I sang of sorrows, failures, fears,
　　And grief the dead past kept.
But those who heard my song of woe
Were sadder as they turned to go!

So then I sang a song of cheer,
　　And people paused and smiled;
I sang of Father's love so dear,
　　And faith of one small child.
Then some who long had ceased to pray
Thanked God and, singing, went their way!
　　　　　　　—4:35 A.M., *Darmstadt, Germany*

Worship

I stood tiptoe upon a little hill,
    And prayer transformed that barren sod.
I can't describe the ecstasy and thrill
    I felt communing there with God.

The holy aim of worship should, forsooth,
    Be "God reseen and man remade,"
Enlarging our dim vision of the truth
    And fitting us for Christ's crusade.

When we insist upon our selfish way—
    A tendency to which we're prone—
It is a mockery to come and pray,
    For we have pushed God from His throne.

If you can come and say with humble heart,
    "I'll choose the will of God as mine,"
You've learned at last the Master's art
    Of living out the life divine.

Ascend each day some mountaintop for prayer
    And take with you all earthly scars.
You'll find when you descend that sacred stair
    You'll walk with head above the stars.

Purpose in Prayer

Our Master climbed the mountaintop to pray,
A wond'rous place to go, but not to stay;
He hastened down—back to the plains again,
To share God's love and healing power with men.

The Master Artist

Who paints the skies at dawn of day?
    It is the Lord.
Why can't I mix my paints that way,
    With such accord?
How can He make the colors blend?
    My colors clash.
I watch but cannot comprehend,
    For He can splash
His colors on the earth or sky,
    Or on the sea,
And they are pleasing to the eye.
    There's harmony.

O God, Thy paintings are divine.
Each flower becomes a wayside shrine!

His Touch Divine

(Inspired by the story of one of Cromwell's officers to whom the
general had just given an important but dangerous assignment.
The officer replied, "I'll go, sir, but before I go, sir, let me feel
the grip of thy conquering hand.")

Dear Lord, I need Thee this new day;
    I need Thee, oh, so much.
Before I venture forth, I pray,
    Please let me feel Thy touch.

I sense Thy holy presence here,
    Put Thou Thy hand on mine.
My graces grow when Thou art near,
    I feel Thy touch divine.

Can anything so well equip
  My life for campaigns planned,
As just to feel the conquering grip
  Of Thy almighty hand?

Written for Our Learning

"For whatsoever things were written aforetime were written for our learning, that we through patience and comfort of the scriptures might have hope." Rom. 15:4.

Ere we complete earth's pilgrimage and walk on streets
  of gold,
We will, like ancient Israel, meet with bitter trials, we're
  told.
For Satan contests ev'ry foot of ground, as on we plod,
Just as he did in ancient times when men would worship
  God.
The first plagues fell upon the Jews as well as on the rest,
And many got discouraged, and they did not stand the test.
But those who trusted God were shown the land of their
  desire,
Although they passed through forty years of crucible by
  fire.
They saw the bitter water at Marah's spring turn sweet.
They saw the smoke of Sinai and worshiped at God's feet.
They heard a voice like thunder, and their hearts were
  filled with awe,
And then they heard the mighty God enunciate the law.
They had to cross the desert and the river Jordan too,
Before their lovely Land of Promise ever came in view.
So some folks got discouraged, and they murmured and
  complained;

They did not like the manna, and the heart of God was
    pained.
They criticized their leaders and they criticized the food,
And criticism left them in a very ugly mood.
Yet Moses still was patient, and the Lord was very kind,
And gave them precious promises to bring them peace
    of mind.
In all their desert wand'rings a remnant did go through,
And made the great discov'ry that God's promises are
    true!
Their weary road was ended, and their suff'rings in the past,
And they rejoiced because they'd reached the Promised
    Land at last!

Receptivity

O God, help me to turn my eyes to Thee,
    Like flowers turn their faces to the sun;
I would reflect Thy light as placid sea
    Reflects the glory of the sky as one.

May I receive Thy light through passing hours,
    As sunbeams, spreading o'er the earth unroll,
Unlock the beauty of the fragrant flowers—
    May Thy love work these wonders in my soul.

I would respond to Thee, like harp to hand,
    Releasing harmonies with heav'nly art;
Like radio in tune with Fatherland,
    Which echoes sweetest songs within my heart.

Awaken sleeping music, Lord, in me,
Through this great gift of receptivity!

Christ Crushed by the Crowd

"He [Jesus] gave directions to His disciples to keep a small boat always ready because of the throng, to prevent their crushing Him." Mark 3:9, Weymouth.

In this mad world of modern man, we meet
Two tragic traffic jams on ev'ry street.
The careless cars that crowd the main highways
Are speeding deathtraps—worse on foggy days.
But there's a greater danger man must face,
For foggy thinking clouds our human race.
The *crowd of things* that keep us occupied,
Leave mind confused and soul unsatisfied.
While smoke and smog help keep man's vision dim,
Cacophony of voices scream at him.
The blare of radios, each neon light,
Demand attention and obscure his sight.
The glaring road signs (and skywriting, too)
All join in telling man what he should do.
Conformity is now the big demand,
And this is true in nearly ev'ry land.
Our lives are standardized by subtle arts—
Mass thinking molds our minds like auto parts.
The advertising world has really sold
Its ounce of drivel for our bag of gold.
TV absorbs the old-time family hour,
And robs the home of this great source of power.
We live forever in a bath of noise,
Which helps disintegrate our peace and poise.
Mere earthly gadgets cannot take the place
Of holy worship's healing power and grace.
In streamlined houses built by modern man,
The dishes may not break, but hearts still can.
Our overcrowded lives and minds, alas,

Are trampled like the crowds who crush the grass.
The grass revives, in time, by gentle showers.
Thus prayer brings man recuperative powers.
Consider all the treasures Christ imparts
When He can dominate our homes and hearts;
All phases of our life Christ must control,
If we iron out the wrinkles of the soul.
We need some quiet time where peace can reign,
For *fog* and *traffic* clutter up the brain!

In many busy lives today, no doubt,
The Christ is being crushed, or crowded out!
—4:15 A.M., *Osaka, Japan*

Insight

When problems come and trials appear,
   With which we have to cope,
A living Faith will banish fear
   And Love will brighten Hope;
For LOVE sees further through a tear
   Than through a telescope!

The Lift of the Tide

As over the ocean of life we ride,
We need the sea breeze and the strong sea tide;
Our stranded adventures—how often they are
Like ships in the grip of a sandy bar.
Ah! then comes the moment we can't conceal—
The ecstatic joy our full hearts feel
When our boats are lifted, again to glide
O'er the swelling seas of the rising tide!

The Morning Watch

This morning e'er the clock struck three
The Lord in love awakened me—
And filled my soul with ecstasy.

For I arose and knelt in prayer
And thanked God for His love and care—
So glad His power is everywhere.

I felt impressed to raise my eyes
And gaze into the starry skies—
Then I was glad He bade me rise.

I saw the blazing suns that shine
With everlasting light divine—
It flooded this poor heart of mine.

A holy peace filled all my soul,
For while I watched the planets roll—
I knew that God is in control!
— 4:39 A.M., *Kuyera, Ethiopia*

Feeding on the Word

He who opens the Scriptures, and feeds upon the heavenly manna, becomes a partaker of the divine nature.—ELLEN G. WHITE in *Review and Herald,* June 28, 1892.

Whoever will open the Sacred Word,
And listen to voices the prophets heard,
Who "hungers and thirsts" and who feels his needs,
And then on this "heavenly manna" feeds,
Partakes of the nature of God divine,
And his thoughts with the thoughts of God combine.

Christ at the Door

"Behold, I stand at the door, and knock.". . . I saw that many have so much rubbish piled up at the door of their heart that they cannot get the door open. Some have difficulties between themselves and their brethren to remove. Others have evil tempers, selfish covetousness, to remove before they can open the door. Others have rolled the world before the door of their heart, which bars the door. All this rubbish must be taken away, and then they can open the door and welcome the Saviour in.—*Testimonies,* vol. 1, p. 143.

Christ knocks each day at our heart's door;
An entrance there He doth implore.
"Behold, I stand and knock," He cries,
With rich rewards for eager eyes.

The faithful Witness counsels all
To hear His voice and heed His call.
For Jesus longs to enter in,
Unless the door is barred with sin.

The rubbish piled up at the door—
We must remove it all before
The door is ever opened wide
To let the blessed Guest inside.

What are the things that block the way,
That dwarf our lives and spoil the day?
Our tantrum tempers, selfishness,
Will bar the way to happiness.

Some roll the world before the door,
With all its subtle, sordid store;
But all this "rubbish" tarred with sin
Must be removed to let Christ in!

Overcrowded Lives

"Jesus had passed out unnoticed, there being a crowd in the place." John 5:13, Weymouth.

In modern man's mad traffic jam
I often wonder where I am.
Has Christ passed from our lives, so proud,
"Unnoticed" midst the madding crowd?

From overcrowded streets we turn
To face what gives us more concern;
The greater problem that I find
Is this—*the overcrowded mind!*

Show windows vie to lure our eyes,
Eclipsing visions of the skies.
In overcrowded stores, 'twould seem,
Materialism reigns supreme.

Along these busy thoroughfares
Ten thousand voices shout their wares.
Like sheep, we follow those who lead;
Confused, buy things we do not need.

The price we pay for "bubbled" bread
Includes the cost of "overhead"
Reflected in each furrowed face—
The "last price" of the market place.

"Be still!" Hear God's voice from the skies.
Prepare to grasp a heav'nly prize.
Earth's static tuned out—that's an *art*
To cure *the overcrowded heart!*

Faith the Builder

Doubt builds no ark;
  Doubt builds no kirk.
Doubt loves the dark;
  Doubt will not work.

Faith turns on light;
  Faith shows the way.
Faith gives us sight;
  Faith saves the day.

Faith blasts doubt's fears;
  Faith's flag's unfurled.
Faith dries doubt's tears;
  Faith saves the world.

Faith builds the roads;
  Faith grasps the hod.
Faith bears life's loads;
  Faith worships God.

Taught of the Lord

It is only at the altar of God that we can kindle our tapers with divine fire.—ELLEN G. WHITE, *Gospel Workers*, p. 255.

We're taught of the Lord in the hour of prayer,
Made stronger the burdens of life to bear.
We rise from our knees released from our sin,
Made wiser and better than we have been.
We go to our work prepared to shine,
By spending this time with our Lord divine.

If Trials Come

If trials ever come to you,
'Twill help to keep the stars in view.
Remember: God knows what to do!

He is not taken by surprise,
So lift your weary, tear-dimmed eyes
And view the glory of the skies.

And though you think things can't be worse,
God soon will end sin's awful curse,
For He still rules the universe!
                —4:20 A.M., *Kuyera, Ethiopia*

Christ, the Wisdom of God

"In whom are hid all the treasures of wisdom and knowledge."
Col. 2:3.
*"But of him are ye in Christ Jesus, who of God is made unto us
wisdom, and righteousness, and sanctification, and redemption."*
1 Cor. 1:30.

How precious are Thy thoughts to us, O God,
    For all creation-manifested thought.
But in the cross was wisdom shed abroad;
    In Christ was God's true wisdom fully taught.

O Christ, I view Thy wounds, Thy bleeding side,
    And kneel beneath Thy cross on holy sod;
Such love and mercy humbles all my pride—
    I see the wisdom and the power of God!

Real Prayer

How many times we "say our prayers"
  As prayer times come and go.
How often do we really pray
  So that our souls can grow?

Do we make worship just a form?
  What is our attitude?
Are we content to merely pray
  Some pretty platitude?

Should not our prayers come from the heart
  Not from our lips alone?
How dare we kneel as though before
  A god of wood or stone?

Real prayer creates an atmosphere
  Of sanctifying grace.
The heart then speaks to our Best Friend—
  O precious trysting place!

Prayer lifts us to a better world,
  That heav'nly world above;
We visit in our Father's house—
  Sweet fellowship of love.

We feel His power in that sweet hour;
  Our hearts He does inspire.
Then we return to earth to "burn"—
  Aflame with holy fire.

3

My Cross

I groaned beneath the burden of my cross,
And reckoned up my bitterness and loss.
I cried, "O God, please take my cross away,
Or let me bear another's cross, I pray."

And so, at last, He granted my request,
And I exchanged my cross as I thought best.
I tried the crosses of my fellow men,
But soon I cried for my cross back again.

I had not known the meaning of the cross,
Or had I plumbed the depth of human dross,
Till through the blessed discipline of pain
I found within the cross my purest gain.

I had not learned the mystery of love,
Or how God prunes the branches from above.
His love divine will spare no fruitful tree,
But prunes that it may yet more fruitful be.

So when upon my cross I saw Christ's face,
I found the secret of His love and grace;
Life's richest gains have come through His great loss—
I've learned at last the meaning of the cross!

Awe

There's mysterious life in every seed,
   Life that is nourished by crumbling clod;
Such power inspires with awe indeed,
   Leads me to worship Almighty God.

The Hand of God

Back of the beauty of earth and sky,
  Back of the surging sea;
Back of the flowers, and birds that fly,
  Back of each fruitful tree;
Back of all glory that greets the eye,
  Back of each mystery;

Back of the gifts of hearing or sight,
  Back of the healing art;
Back of the precious boon of light
  And blessing it doth impart;
Back of the lifting laws of right,
  Back of each transformed heart;

Back of the atom's infinite power,
  Back of the lightning's rod;
Back of the fragrance of ev'ry flower,
  Back of the seed and sod;
Back of the sun and refreshing shower,
  I see the hand of God.

Living Epistles

What God could not say through the language of man,
He said through a Life in a far-better plan.
The Word was made flesh in that wonderful birth,
To dwell among people who lived on the earth.
For men misinterpret the words that we give,
But can't misinterpret the lives that we live.
So Jesus must live in our own hearts again,
That the Word then made flesh may still dwell among men!

The Meaning of the Cross

When to our trembling lips
    The bitter cup of woe is pressed,
        And we must taste life's gall with briny tears;
And trials come to crush our ships
    With fierce and fiery test,
        And make us captives of our doubts and fears—

'Tis then, sometimes, we see
    Another's sorrow, suff'ring pain
        So piercing as to shame our selfish thought
Of our own destiny,
    And flashes flame across our brain,
        Dwarfing our petty tragedies to nought!

So when you're tempted sore
    To ask the everlasting "Why?"
        Then think of Job and all who've suffered loss,
Or, climb up Calv'ry's hill once more,
    And watch your Saviour die,
        And learn anew the meaning of the cross!

Our Rendezvous With God

"Truly our fellowship is with the Father, and with his Son Jesus Christ." 1 John 1:3.

From hours spent with God He came forth morning by morning, to bring the light of heaven to men. Daily He received a fresh baptism of the Holy Spirit. In the early hours of the new day the Lord awakened Him from His slumbers, and His soul and His lips were anointed with grace, that He might impart to others. —*Christ's Object Lessons,* p. 139.

I met with God at dawn today,
And watched the stars all fade away;
And in the hush and blush of morn,
I stood entranced while day was born.
God draws so very near at dawn,
While curtains of the day are drawn.
These precious early morning hours
Replenish all man's nobler powers,
The finest time of day, it seems,
For worship and for holy themes.
From nature's book, not writ with pen,
I learn my daily lesson then.

The rising sun with sheer delight
Bombards the earth with darts of light,
And all of nature feels the thrill
Of power that moves from hill to hill.
And from the darkened vales below
We see the beacon lights aglow
On ev'ry radiant mountain peak.
'Tis then we kneel, too stirred to speak;
We wait in reverential awe,
As sun, ablaze, obeys God's law,
And in three minutes' time, they say,
That sun will quietly convey
More power to earth, in heat and light,
Than all the coal man burns (that's right),
More than the coal, in one whole year,
Produces for his uses here!
God's power is free and blesses earth,
Yet who can estimate its worth?
How few take time to thank the God
Who sheds such energy abroad?

So in this early morning hour,
While nature throbs with mighty power,
We feel a stir within our hearts,
As God bombards our souls with darts
Of love and light, and we are thrilled,
Our minds with inspiration filled!
How can man sleep through such an hour
When God releases all this power?
Awake, O Christian, meet thy tryst,
And fellowship with God and Christ.
What greater thing is there to do
Than *keep this daily rendezvous?*
                    —*Addis Ababa, Ethiopia*

Lend Me Your Ear

"Be still and know that I am God." Ps. 46:10.

A thousand voices clamor for your ear,
But only you decide what you will hear.
Above this earthly din, God says, "Be still,"
But He will never force the human will.
As long as God is God and man is man,
You must decide—there is no other plan!

Be Hopeful

"I go straight for the goal." Phil. 3:13, 14, Phillips translation.

Arise! Lift up your eager eyes!
    With faces forward, move ahead.
Each dawn expect some fresh surprise,
    And never greet the day with dread.

Why should we let our sorrows last?
  Each day's mistakes we must forget.
Save only fire from out the past,
  And not the ashes of regret.

Life's Great Decision

"What shall I do then with Jesus which is called Christ?" Matt.
27:22.

When Pilate said, "What shall I do with Christ?"
He made his great decision while enticed
By popularity, and compromised
With principle—but while he temporized
He toyed too long with conscience and with truth,
As many adults since, and many youth,
Have done to their eternal loss,
And crucified the Christ upon the cross!

Is destiny decided by one act,
By what we do when faced with some great fact?
Will we be judged by God's all-searching eye
By what *we* do with truth or with a lie?
"What shall I do with Christ?" Each must decide.
He waits our answer. Can He be denied?

Oh, let's decide for Christ and stand with Him
Lest earth-born clouds should make *our* vision dim.
Make your decision now, decide today
To walk with Christ along His living way.
With Christ we have *an endless hope,* my friend,
Without Christ we will have *a hopeless end!*
                    —4:00 A.M., *Tegucigalpa, Honduras*

Christ Did Not Fail

"He shall not fail nor be discouraged." Isa. 42:4.

Christ did not fail, though Satan did his worst;
Christ did not fail, though men and demons cursed;
He did not fail because His faith was strong;
He did not fail, but sang the victor's song!

We must not fail or weaken in the fight;
We dare not fail to spread the gospel light;
How can we fail? Christ says, "I'll go with you!"
We will not fail, because His word is true!

"There Is a Balm in Gilead"

The days ahead will teach us things
　　As yet man never knew.
Time will assuage the bitter stings
　　Which now are hurting you.
The future's rich rewards of worth
　　Will end the pain you feel;
There is no sorrow on this earth
　　Which Heaven cannot heal.

Soul on Fire

The greatest books—the books that most inspire—
Are penned by men who write with soul on fire.
When such a vivid flame shines on their theme
They write with pen dipped in a living stream.

SECTION 2

At Work With God

Crusading With Christ

We'll march in zeal with flags unfurled,
   We'll go with feet well shod;
We'll take the truth to all the world,
   And share our faith in God!

Inspired by Paul

"Let us be Christ's men from head to foot and give no chances to the flesh to have its fling!" Rom. 13:11-14, Phillips translation.

I love to read the letters of the great apostle Paul.
He wrote so many of them from within a prison wall.
He did not get discouraged, or resign himself to fate,
Or say, "There's nothing I can do," then sit and vegetate.
He found his work in prison and he learned the power of
    prayer.
While in the jail in Philippi he won the jailer there.
He spent much time in study for he wrote, "Bring me the
    books!"
And did not whine about hard beds or criticize the cooks.
No murm'ring word about how *dark* and *cold* the dungeon
    stones,
Just "Bring my coat e'er winter comes"—to shield his
    shiv'ring bones!
He made those stones his pulpit where he gave a clarion
    call—
Those years he spent in prison were the greatest years of
    all!
He penned his grand epistles and they throb with mighty
    power,
The Spirit of the living God sustained him hour by hour.

If soft and flabby Christians in this modern world we know,
Would leave their television sets (and also radio),
And spend a year in jail with Paul and hear this great
    man's voice,
It would revive the church on earth and heaven would re-
    joice.

Earth's time-consuming gadgets rob the church of much
    manpower:
Why, some folks sit and listen to the TV by the hour!
Their eyes bulge out with wonder; soon they'll have a
    new disease,
With eyes the size of cantaloupes and brains like small
    split peas.
You do not have to use your mind, just sit—be entertained:
Most programs, geared to ten-year-olds, will please the
    scatterbrained!
But since we have a mission with a mighty work to do,
Be careful how you spend your time and what you listen to.
Of all the talents God has giv'n, of none will He require
A reckoning as strict as of our time! So, I inquire,
How do you spend your leisure time? What is your lifetime
    goal?
Is your time spent in worldliness or helping win a soul?
Don't say there's nothing you can do—remember Paul
    in jail—
Just go to work right where you are and you will never fail.
Go find the brokenhearted; let the love of God be shown.
Go share your precious faith; the soul you save may be
    your own.

                —5:00 A.M., *Bergen, Norway*

Sermons Seen

Lives of loyal laymen fire us
    With their holy zeal divine—
All their thrilling deeds inspire us,
    We must likewise rise and shine!

"What Is That in Thine Hand?"

I've heard it said that Gypsy Smith found joy
In shaking hands with ev'ry little boy.
An eager mother brought her son one night,
To introduce him to "the man of light."
The little fellow held his left hand out,
While on his face there was a tell-tale pout.
So Gypsy smiled and took a different tack,
When Johnny hid his hand behind his back.
The great evangelist then took his stand,
And said, "My little man, where's your right hand?"

Reluctantly the lad held out his right,
But that right hand was really clenched up tight.
Then Gypsy said, "I cannot understand
Why you don't open up and shake my hand."
The boy looked in the preacher's face with dread,
"I can't: I've got some marbles there," he said.

He missed the chance to grasp that hand of power
Because he held those playthings of the hour.
How many times we see someone who clings
With fierce tenacity to earthly things.
How many folks are like that little boy!
They fail because their hands have clutched some toy.
They cannot grasp the hand of Christ, the King,
Because they won't let go of some plaything.

What occupies your time and thought, I pray?
Are your hands busy with God's work each day?
What would you answer Him if Christ should stand
And ask you what you're holding in your hand?

A Prayer to Be Adequate

(Inspired by the famous comment on prayer by Phillips Brooks.)

Dear God, we do not pray for easy lives,
But to be stronger men, with greater drives.
We do not merely pray, through passing hours,
For tasks we think are equal to our powers.
Instead, we come to Thee, O God, to ask
For powers to make us equal to our task!

Hands

Hands, in man's art,
Reflect his heart.
  If good or bad,
  If glad or sad.
    By day or night,
    For wrong or right,
      The hands of man
      Work out some plan.
        Hands state his case
        More than his face.

Our hands convey
What we can't say.
  Our hands caress;
  Our hands can bless.
    Our hands are tools
    For wise or fools.
      At work or play,
      By night, by day,
        Hands work the sod;
        Hands worship God.

The Secret of Persuasive Power

The deeds of history books which stir mankind
Vibrated first within the author's mind.
And he who writes of rivers must take pains
To feel the river flowing through his veins.

Since we must preach Christ's gospel to the poles,
HIS story first must vibrate in our souls.
No one describes God's love with winsome art
Unless that love is surging in his heart!

The Story of the Coward and the Hero

A story Edward Sill once told
　　Fired men with veneration.
This tale deserves to be retold
　　And stir our generation.

A coward paused at battle's edge—
　　Defeated by his attitude!
He failed his Prince, forgot his pledge—
　　Revealed his base ingratitude.

He cried, "How can I be of aid
　　With this poor, crude accouterment?
The Prince no doubt wields blue-steel blade—
　　But see my clumsy instrument.

"For this old sword I hold in hand
　　Should be a baby's rattle."
He broke it, flung it in the sand,
　　And then—ran from the battle.

The Prince possessed no blue-steel blade,
　Yet he fought on with empty hands.
He would not let his courage fade
　Though pushed back, bleeding, o'er the sands.

He stumbled o'er the broken sword,
　The sword the coward had thrown away.
He grasped the hilt, his courage soared—
　He charged—and won the war that day.

He charged—his deed was so adored,
　His soldiers fought with all their soul.
That hero with but half a sword
　Did more than "coward" could with whole.

He Won the Last One

George Washington, the story goes, and we are told it's
　right,
Lost twenty-seven battles but he would not cease to fight.
Although his soldiers struggled on in tattered clothes and
　shoes,
And though they fought in ice and snow, he vowed they
　could not lose.
He knelt in prayer at Valley Forge and sought the help of
　God,
And soon his faith and courage and his spirit spread abroad.
The army and the nation then arose as one strong man,
Responded to his leadership and followed out his plan.
They all fought on, they would not quit until the war was
　won.
George lost a score of battles but *he won the last big one!*

Real or Self-made Martyrs?

*I thank God for my handicaps, for through them I have found myself, my work, and my God.—*HELEN KELLER.

Along earth's journey, strewn with strife,
   I've watched with keenest concentration
The way folks meet the trials of life—
   It's been a mighty revelation!

Some face their problems with a smile,
   And work with cheerful animation;
And from each trial, in ev'ry mile,
   They somehow find fresh inspiration.

These are the Helen Keller type,
   They take what comes, and don't collapse;
They do not grovel, grieve, or gripe,
   But thank God for their handicaps.

They learn from what Miss Keller said,
   That handicaps are man's best prod;
And through these problems most men dread,
   They find themselves, their work, their God!

Another type just sits and mourns,
   And sings a song of lamentation;
Some wear a self-made crown of thorns—
   The self-made martyrs of each nation!
             —Nov. 10, 1963, 4:40 A.M.
             Debra Tabor, Ethiopia

What Is Happiness?

Is happiness that holy light
   That gladdens sight,
   And shines so bright
   In earth's dark night
      From the *burning* candle of love?

Is happiness that music sweet
   With rhythmic beat
   We sometimes meet
   On life's sad street,
      From the *throbbing* bells of love?

Is happiness that perfume rare,
   Beyond compare,
   Spread everywhere,
   By those who care,
      From the *bruised* rose of love?

Is happiness that hope serene
   Which we may glean
   When we have seen
   What crosses mean,
      From the *dying* Christ of love?

Yes, light is sweet, yet the candle consumes;
Roses are crushed to release their perfumes.
Bells must be beaten to vibrate and ring;
Christ through His cross makes our happy hearts sing!

4

Salute to Laymen

We hail the loyal laymen who have heard
  The voice of Christ who pleads with love divine;
These heroes come, obedient to His Word,
  Responding to His call to rise and shine.

They swell the laymen's army in its might;
  They lift the torch of truth at home, abroad;
They find a thousand ways to *send the light*
  And help enlarge the kingdom of our God.

The burning passion of His larger claim
  Inspires and fires their souls to nobler deeds,
And puts all doubts and selfishness to shame,
  For they are meeting mankind's deepest needs.

They feel the pull of everlasting power,
  The mighty magnet of a higher goal,
For they have seen the challenge of the hour—
  The vision of the value of a soul.

May God accept and bless each flaming heart
  Whose shining service is of priceless worth,
As each one finds his place and plays his part
  To finish God's great work upon the earth.

Patience

I want to be a patient, true promoter,
  And calmly bear life's burden of the years—
For patience is the idling of the motor—
  Instead of madly stripping all the gears!

Salt of the Earth

The Master said that salt is good
　　'Till it has lost its savor.
'Tis then insipid in our food,
　　Devoid of taste or flavor.

What does this word *insipid* mean?
　　It means no taste, just flat or stale,
No freshness or no sparkle keen,
　　But thin and weak and dull and pale.

A Christian is the "salt of earth,"
　　With tang and animation;
His sparkle is of priceless worth
　　In mankind's preservation!

Action or Inaction?

There's nothing quite so tragic, Goethe said,
　　As *"ignorance* in action." (What a sight!)
But without works, James wrote, your faith is dead—
　　That's *knowledge* with inaction. (Gives no light!)

To know and not to tell what we have learned
　　Can never meet God's purpose or desire;
How dare we wait till someone's house has burned,
　　Then tell him that we knew it was on fire.

Go! Wage a holy war against all wrong;
　　This is the task of adults and of youth.
Go! Sing it if you know a lovely song;
　　Go! Share it if you know God's precious truth!

The Consecrated Car

She was not the gifted kind,
But only one of humble mind.
Yet she became our shining star—
She had a consecrated car!

When we had work, though small or grand,
She was the first to raise her hand
And volunteer to use her car,
And never asked how close or far.

There were so many things we knew
That this dear member could not do;
But she would say, "I'll use my car
And bring my friends from near and far."

And though she could not sing or speak,
She brought her thirteen ev'ry week.
How many trips she made each night!
It was her way to "spread the light."

And when the effort closed that year
The harvest brought much holy cheer;
She saw her thirteen baptized too,
And proved there's something each can do!

That's how she was our shining star—
She had a consecrated car.
She must have had Christ's spirit too—
With all she had she followed through.

Our Missionary Magazines

How can we answer the world's crying need—
  The need of the aged and the youth?
Send out the *Signs of the Times* which will feed
  Earth's heart-hungry folks with the truth.

Send out the *Message* while men still may read—
  Remember our soul-winning goals.
Circulate *Message*—this journal will plead
  With millions of judgment-bound souls.

Mail out *These Times* to each neighbor and friend—
  The seeds of the truth must be sown.
Rush them *These Times,* knowing time soon will end;
  Your life's harvest then will be shown!

What Will You Give?

When Abraham first heard God's call
  At once he broke all worldly ties;
He turned his back upon it all
  For that new home above the skies.

When Jesus left His throne on high
  He came to seek and save the lost;
To save our souls He had to die!
  Did He refuse to count the cost?

What will *you* give to save lost men?
  What vision looms before your eyes?
Will *your* gifts help Christ come again?
  What will *you* give in sacrifice?

The Fountain

How faithfully the fountain draws its water, clear and clean,
From never-failing sources, with its crystal, silv'ry sheen.
It gives its liquid treasure to enrich our life and health,
And yet, man never can compute its value or its wealth.

I wish that I could emulate this pure, life-giving spring,
And spend my lifetime giving, too, and, like it, sweetly sing.
"O Fountain, do you ever tire and wish the stream would
    cease?"
"Oh, no," it cried, "I share my blessings; therefore I have
    peace."

"While the Angels Hold the Four Winds"

While the angels hold the four winds, we are to work with all
our capabilities. We must bear our message without any delay.—
Testimonies, vol. 6, p. 21.

Dark storm clouds thrashing in the western sky,
    With thunder clashing, crashing in great power,
And lightning dashing, lashing, seem to vie
    With setting sun—all flashing time's last hour!

But hark! A voice is heard above the din.
    The voice of God cries, "Hold the winds of strife,
Till all My saints are sealed and saved from sin,
    That they through Christ may gain eternal life."

So while the angels hold the winds of war,
    We now must work with greater zeal and love,
Proclaiming truth more fully near and far—
    All men must hear God's message from above!

Joseph

"This dreamer comes," his jealous brothers said;
But later Joseph fed them all with bread.
For Joseph caught a vision of his God
And served Him well at home and when abroad.

He always sought to know and do God's will,
And from the hate of man pure love distill.
He kept his body fit for God to use;
Whenever urged to sin, he would refuse.

His life was always safe within God's hand,
Although the trials he could not understand;
But he'd resolved to God he would be true,
And faithful be in all he had to do.

He walked with God, the One he'd learned to know,
And so to each temptation he said No.
His faith in God no woe could ever shake.
God blessed the whole wide world for Joseph's sake.

The world now needs more dreamers like this man,
To live for God and help fulfill His plan!

Worry, a Killer

Blind worry quickly wears away
    The forces of our life.
Unfits us for the fight of day,
    Unnerves us for the battle's strife,
    And murders like a knife.

Oh, worry is a caustic thing,
    It burns and sears the soul;
It robs the heart of songs to sing,
    Eclipsing ev'ry worthy goal,
    And steals our self-control.
            —3:30 A.M., *Debra Tabor, Ethiopia*

Reformers

"Ye are the light of the world;
 Ye are the salt of the earth."
Christ wants His banner unfurl'd;
Truth demands sharing its worth.

What will we do with our light?
How will we lighten each town?
When will we serve with our might?
Who will soon claim heaven's crown?

God's Lamplighters

The eventide of Time is here;
    Dense, dismal darkness wraps the world in night.
Our task is clear—spread cheer this year.
    As God's lamplighters, *flood the world with light!*

God's Book imparts this sacred art;
    Our smiling eyes will radiate God's love;
Each hand and heart must play its part
    To light earth's lamps with fresh fire from above!

Good Samaritans Live Again

Good Samaritans live again,
Bringing comfort and strength to men;
Breaking chains of doubt and fear,
Sharing their love, their hope and cheer.

Good Samaritans understand
How to use the helping hand,
How to meet each human need,
By their service live their creed.

Good Samaritans soon will know
What their fruits of service show,
For in heaven they will find
Rich rewards for being kind.

How to Reach a Goal

We need the help of a faithful guide;
We need the lift of the rising tide.
We need the speed of a steady gale;
We need a compass to set the sail.

We need direction! Oh, set your soul
And feel the pull of a higher goal.
Don't be content with what you've done,
But hitch your chariot to the sun.

Pursue your aim with your ev'ry breath—
An aimless life is a living death!

The Measure of the Man

William James, the great psychologist, said the average person does not utilize more than 10 per cent of his potential powers.

Great difficulties make great men;
From struggle comes our strength.
No man was ever greater than
His battles won at length.

Small difficulties make small men;
When trials come, be glad.
Our struggles call forth hidden powers
We never knew we had.

Few men use more than 10 per cent
Of their potential power.
May God inspire us all to meet
The challenge of this hour.

We must complete the worldwide task
God gave the church to do;
And to this greatest work on earth,
Each member must be true.

When we love God with all our heart,
We reach life's highest goal;
The measure of surrender is
The measure of the soul.

The Christian Way

Within our modern caravansary
Few catch the genius of the Christian way.

A Cry in the Night

I heard it, or it may have been a dream
(It's passing strange how real a dream can seem)—
I heard a call, a voice cried out last night,
"Give us your faith, your hope, your light."
I said, "Who art thou? Why disturb my sleep?"
He cried, "My name is Legion and our needs are deep.
I represent the millions everywhere
Who walk in darkness and in deep despair.
We are the lost of earth, yet no one cares.
Our hearts are bare, though some are millionaires.
We've tried men's panaceas in their turn,
But none gives lasting peace, so now we yearn
To know if you have light from God; we plead,
Give us the answer to our deepest need."

I rose there in the darkness from my bed
And fell upon my knees in holy dread.
I prayed, "O God, what can I say or do?"
He said, "Go, tell the vision shown to you."
And so this day I pass on this appeal
To every Christian heart who still can feel
And hear this modern Macedonian call
That comes from out earth's darkness like a pall.
The church must now "arise" and truly "shine,"
For this is Heaven's purpose and design.
While angels hold the winds of war and strife
Let's quickly give the world God's words of life.
Let's hear the call that comes each day and night:
"Give us your faith, your hope, your light."

The Adequate Man

"Not that we are sufficient of ourselves to think any thing as of ourselves; but our sufficiency is of God." 2 Cor. 3:5.

The adequate man is the rare man who gives
The treasures of life by the way that he lives.
He does not rest satisfied merely to *find*,
But God's blessings flow through his heart and his mind.

The man who is empty finds life empty too,
And chaotic hearts have no calm rendezvous.
The man who gains mast'ry in all of earth's strife
Is one who enthrones Christ as Master of life.
Beset by temptations in this world of sin,
His faith is sufficient, for Christ reigns within.

Since God measures men by the size of their prayers,
The adequate man has the spirit that cares.
He prays for the lost and the lonely of earth;
His sensitive soul is of infinite worth.
The service he renders is not by the clock;
A spiritual seismograph, feeling the shock,
The pain, and the sorrow of each broken heart,
And serving mankind with a heaven-born art.

With adequate faith and with adequate love,
With adequate wisdom from Heaven above,
With adequate patience and adequate grace,
With adequate charm and a smile on his face,
And adequate courage, he matches each need
With adequate strength and with adequate deed.

Oh, who is sufficient for life such as this,
The ultimate, surely, of true happiness?
In view of these times, of our needs, and Thy plan,
O God, canst Thou make me an adequate man?

The Sabbath School Teacher

The teacher's task upon this earth
Is measureless in terms of worth.
With wisdom, tact, and patient art,
He guides the human mind and heart.
Man's works of art in stone or clay
The ravages of time decay;
But he who molds the mind of man
According to the Master's plan,
Performs a deed which long will last
When other things on earth have passed.
So let us magnify this task—
Is there a greater work? I ask.

Since we agree this work is great,
What else on earth can compensate
If we neglect to do the thing
Which does so many blessings bring?
For ev'ry student, young or old,
Is dearer far than purest gold
To teachers who have hearts that burn
With faith and love and deep concern!
So dedicate your life anew
To grandest work that man can do,
As ev'ry Sabbath day you seize
These weekly opportunities!

"It Pleased God . . ."

"God hath chosen the weak things of the world to confound the things that are mighty."—1 Cor. 1:27.

God chooses humble men and meek
    To match the proud and strong;
He calls the "weakest of the weak"
    To rout the hosts of wrong.

God uses base and foolish things
    Confounding wise and great;
Sometimes a simple statement brings
    Their doom and seals their fate.

If God chose stronger men to fight
    Against strong men, so tough,
The strong might think they still were right,
    But not quite strong enough.

If God chose wiser men to meet
    The wisdom of the wise,
They yet might be, in their defeat,
    Still wise in their own eyes.

But when God shakes the wise and strong
    With humble souls and weak,
We know to whom the thanks belong—
    For God works through the meek.

No man dares glory in God's sight,
    Or walk with haughty eyes;
Through humble folk God takes delight
    To shame the worldly wise!

                —3:30 A.M., at *Bo, Sierra Leone*

The Call of Duty

The open roads of earth say "Go."
  The comfort of my home says "Stay."
It's pleasant in my house, I know;
  But, I must leave and go away.

A million hungry children call;
  I hear their piercing, pleading cries.
I go to seek and find them all,
  To save each one before he dies.

And so I tear myself away
  From warmth and joys of fireside's glow,
Though all my selfish soul says "Stay,"
  I hear the voice of God say "Go."

"Save Me From Myself"

St. Augustine, so long ago,
Discussed the depths of human woe.
He saw the devil's fiendish art
In tempting ev'ry human heart.
He saw how weak, depraved, is man,
In yielding to the devil's plan,
And cried out, in his earthly pelf,
"God, save me from my sinful self."

A second danger that I face,
When God has saved me by His grace,
And He has rescued me from sin,
And I the Christian race begin;
I look upon the motley crowd,

And I become so very proud
Of all the virtuous deeds I do.
God, save me from this "good man" too.

For we become so proud of race,
Or feel a sense of pride of place;
And we can get so proud of face,
And even proud of all our grace;
Of pride there must be left no trace,
When Christ, the Judge, decides my case!

God's Finished Work

G—God has a mighty work that must be done.
O—Only a little time ere set of sun.
D—Doing this work is the challenge we face;
S—Surely each Christian must now find his place.

F—Final events will be rapid, we know.
I—Infinite power the Lord will bestow.
N—Now let's redouble our efforts and will,
I—In faithful service God's plan to fulfill.
S—Speed on the truth—let us coordinate—
H—Help give God's message before it's too late.
E—Each must cooperate, visit each home,
D—Daringly witness wherever we roam.

W—Waiting and working, faithful and true,
O—One goal—a finished work—always in view.
R—Revitalized by the Spirit's power,
K—Kept by His grace and matched for this hour!

SECTION 3

Over the Parapets of the World

O'er Parapets of the World

Come, walk with me o'er ramparts of the world,
And see the banner of the Lord unfurl'd.
We'll find the footprints of a loyal band
Of those who serve in ev'ry mission land.
We'll count the graves o'er which wild flowers have
     grown—
Someday the glorious harvest will be known.

A Vision in the Austrian Alps

(Inspired by Ezekiel 40:2-4, opening text used at the Laymen's Convention at Schladming, Austria, 1960.)

Schladming is in the center of the Austrian wonderland,
The mountain peaks in splendor beckon with a rugged
    hand.
We heard those mountains calling and responded to their
    call,
And we beheld the beauty of each sparkling waterfall.
The music of the water, flowers smiling from the sod—
We heard the voice of nature—Oh, we heard the voice of
    God!
        Blessed were our ears, for they heard!
        Many go and never hear a word,
        Or if they do, they only hear a bird.

We saw the tow'ring mountain peaks point upward to the
    skies,
And we beheld a grandeur rarely seen by human eyes.
The sky was blue as indigo, adorned with fleecy clouds;
We climbed so high above the world and all its madding
    crowds,
Until we saw majestic scenes where man has never trod,
And we beheld a vision—Oh, we saw a glimpse of God!
        Blessed were our eyes—they saw the King!
        Many look and never see a thing,
        Or only pause to hear a wild bird sing.

We felt a holy presence in that awe-inspiring hour.
We sensed the strength of mountains and an overwhelming
    power.

We paused in purest worship—ev'ry breath became a
   prayer;
And so we breathed the deeper of that clear, pure mountain
   air.
It was effulgent glory rising from the Alpine sod.
We felt a holy presence—Oh, we felt the power of God!
      Blessed were our hearts, renewed with power,
      We cherish mem'ries of that holy hour.
      Many go and only find a flower!
                  —4:09 A.M., *Schladming, Austria*

Bermuda—Enchanted Isle

Like a string of pearls in a shining sea,
   Is Bermuda, pride of the ocean;
Her waving palms sing a song to the free,
   And kindle the heart's devotion.

Her silver sands smoothed by soft, silent tides,
   Caressed by the warmth of the sun,
Produce a peace where nature confides
   Some secrets so dear to each one.

The ships that were sunk—a hundred or more—
   With stirring tales these reefs are rife.
What voices we hear when winter winds roar—
   Romantic adventures of life.

The charm of Bermuda—increase her tribe—
   The people who know how to smile;
We've found hidden treasures we can't describe—
   Bermuda, the Enchanted Isle!

The Call of the American Indians

At last we hear a cry for help that comes to you and me
From neighbors just as needy as our brothers o'er the sea.
The Indians of America are stretching out their hands
To grasp the truths of Christ just like the folks in mission
    lands.

Just recently a Navaho—a drunkard, so they say—
Received a most impressive dream that made him kneel
    and pray.
He saw the heavens open, and he saw Christ come again,
Observed how all the Navahos became fear-ridden men;
They cried for rocks and mountains to hide them from
    God's face,
But saw the Sabbathkeeping Christians saved by God's
    great grace.

This dream was so impressive that he told it everywhere,
And many Indians have been led to turn to God in prayer.
Just recently this convert and twenty others, too,
Received the rite of baptism—it thrilled us through and
    through.
The hand of God is working; the task will soon be done;
So we must do our duty before the set of sun.

It's our responsibility to spread the truth abroad,
And gather in the lost of earth—each straying child of
    God.
And in this happy family the Indians must have part;
Will you now love them with your means and also with
    your heart?

The Scoffer

He scoffs at scars,
　　Who never felt a spear;
He laughs at grief,
　　Who never shed a tear.
He sneers at pain,
　　Who never needed balm;
He mocks at God,
　　Who never felt His calm!

Self-pity

Shun self-pity as you would shun the leprosy.—MURIEL LESTER.

Lo! Pity is a lovely stream,
　　When flowing out to others.
We see its sparkling, shining gleam
　　In sympathy of mothers.

But pity, when it turns to self,
　　Becomes a vile and stagnant pool;
For kindness hoarded on a shelf,
　　Turns to corruption as a rule.

Self-pity hastens your collapse,
　　For you have lost your self-control.
Oh! Shun self-pity for its saps
　　Your strength, defeats the noblest soul!

A man feels sorry for himself in vain,
With everything to lose and nought to gain!
　　　　　　　　—*Debra Tabor, Ethiopia*

Along Korean Roads

We drove along Korean roads
Where workmen bear tremendous loads
Upon their heads and on their backs—
Their crops and wares make heavy packs.
Most people walk the roads in white
Though some are robed in colors bright.
And student uniforms of blue
Enhance the beauty of the view.
Wild cosmos bloom along the way
In many colors bright and gay.
The peaceful valleys so serene
Present the annual harvest scene.
The good earth yields its crops of gold
And all take part—the young and old.
They thresh with care the golden grain
In time to miss the winter rain.
When crops are gathered in and dried,
The farmers' hopes seem satisfied,
While bright-red peppers add their charm
To every village home and farm.
You see them drying in the sun,
Which means the harvesttime is done.
Rich apples and persimmons red,
Of which enough cannot be said;
And large round pears with nectar sweet
Add flavor to the food you eat.
The cabbage and the rice are stored,
The radishes and all the hoard
Of things they need with which to make
The *kemchi* which they love to take.
These patient people never tire—

They are a race you must admire.
And since we went to On Min Do
And saw the love they can bestow,
I have a feeling I will share—
In God's great kingdom they'll be there.

Borneo

Around the earth, as it forever whirls,
Are many island gems, like precious pearls,
Which sparkle in the shining Southern seas,
And Borneo is surely one of these.
Except for Greenland and New Guinea's girth,
It is the largest island on the earth.
The equatorial line runs through the isle,
So you are in the tropics all the while.
Its sandy shores are laved by Southern seas,
So you will welcome each refreshing breeze.
The Dyaks, Dusans, Ibans, form the race,
Which very largely occupy the place.
And several million people now live here,
Where once head-hunters spread perennial fear.
This is the place orangutans still grow,
And that word means "wild man" of Borneo.
The jungles of the island are quite thick,
And worse to penetrate than walls of brick.
Whole villages still live in their longhouse,
With many families, each man and his spouse.
With many hills the island is replete,
And boasts one mountain thirteen thousand feet.
The peaks of Kinabalu look serene,
But snow upon the peaks is never seen.
And from our school on Tamparuli's height,

The mount, by moonlight, was a glorious sight.
'Twas here at dawn I stood beside the door
To hear bird songs I never heard before.
But also sights and songs of greater worth—
Our Christian youth, the richest prize on earth!
                                        —*Borneo, 1961*

The Canadian Rockies

From Jasper to Banff an extravaganza
of breath-taking beauty!

Colossal mountains pierce the azure sky;
Stupendous peaks whose granite fingers vie
To paint grand pictures for each passer-by.

What rich and rugged grandeur grips our gaze
And leaves us stagg'ring mid the glorious maze;
Such breathless beauty prompts perennial praise!

What fiery cauldrons boiled this molten mass?
Now shining glaciers crown each tow'ring pass,
Whose blue-green depths are seen in each crevasse.

Some lofty peaks with diadems of snow
Are mirrored in the crystal lakes below
Or canyons where the milky rivers flow.

All this majestic beauty spreads abroad,
With mountain flowers smiling from the sod;
In all we trace the fingerprints of God!

Where Byron Wrote

(We visited the Chateau of Chillon while in Europe. We went down into the dungeon and found that Byron had carved his name in the rock during his incarceration there. That night we slept in the hotel where Byron wrote his poem "The Prisoner of Chillon." The occasion awakened the muse in me, and I wrote these lines:)

This is the house where Byron wrote
  "The Prisoner of Chillon."
He found a mental antidote
  For all he'd looked upon.

This is the lake, still as serene
  As when it bathed his eyes;
These are the tow'ring Alps, so clean,
  Still pointing to the skies.

We saw the chateau yesterday,
  And dungeon in the rock,
Where Byron saw men pine away,
  Crushed 'neath their mental shock.

There in the stone we saw his name—
  For Byron carved it deep—
He'd seen and felt the bitter shame
  That made those strong men weep.

He peered out through those prison bars—
  That little hole of light—
He'd climbed that wall to see the stars,
  Enraptured by the sight.

He looked out through that iron grate
   And gazed on mountain peaks;
He felt the irony of fate—
   But lo! the prisoner speaks:

"I saw them—and they were the same;
They were not changed, like me, in frame;
I saw their thousand years of snow
On high—their wide, long lake below,
And the blue Rhone in fullest flow;
I heard the torrents leap and gush
O'er channeled rock and broken bush."

That is the way all prisoners feel,
   Who, groping, find a light.
When will the church heed the appeal
   Of ev'ry prisoner's plight?

Millions of men in darkness still
   Need light for blinded eyes;
Let's open windows so they'll thrill
   With a divine surprise!
            —4:00 A.M., *Lake Geneva, Switzerland*

Laymen Lead the Way

Around the world, we're proud to say,
Our loyal laymen lead the way;
Where'er we go in mission lands
The laymen serve with helping hands.

The laymen who are Spirit-filled,
And in their classes are well drilled,

Become a mighty force for good
And form a blessed brotherhood.

Their lives are fragrant, like a flower,
And measureless their lifting power,
For ten times greater is their reach
Than greatest sermons preachers preach.

They give their talents and their time
To do the work of God sublime.
They fill a universal need—
God's men of destiny indeed!

Tropical Treasures

There's buried beauty in these Southern seas,
    Unseen by casual eyes;
But he who looks beneath the surface sees
    A photographic prize.

This isle is one of thousands that God made
    To make His wonders known;
We found its water wonderland displayed
    A glory all its own.

Just as desert blossoms that bloom unseen
    Seem wasted in the air,
Likewise these coral islands so serene
    Hold gems beyond compare.

I do not speak of chests of pirate's gold,
    But things of greater worth;

You are, while watching all this wealth unfold,
    The richest man on earth.

The problems of this tortured world depart,
    As you relax awhile;
The treasures of contentment flood your heart,
    While on this tropic isle!
                 —3:30 A.M., *Djakarta, Indonesia*

The World's Slow Stain

Beware of the contagion of the world's slow stain;
Beware of the allurement of every temp'ral gain;
Beware of all temptations before your carnal eyes;
For you've eternal treasures waiting in the skies!

O Christian, shut your eye-gate to sordid things of earth,
And keep your ear-gate open to hear God's words of worth.
It's not enough to slap your hand, like Johnny did, and say,
"Don't eat those cookies, Johnny," but eat them anyway.

For Johnny never tried to be more than halfway good.
He showed respect for moral law—as we know well he
    should—
Then tried to ease his conscience by slapping his own hand,
But held on to the cooky jar just as he had planned.

O Christian, flee temptation, and forsake enchanted ground,
And break through sin's contamination which has had you
    bound.
Beware of the allurement of every earthly gain;
Beware of the contagion of the world's slow stain.

SECTION 4

Aspiration

Think

Oh, think great thoughts, think noble themes,
For when a man no longer dreams,
Or sees no vision in the sky,
He then and there begins to die!

The Lincoln Memorial

What do we see in Lincoln's form and face?
Mere marble loveliness and sculptured grace?
Much more! We see a poem carved in stone;
We see a moral giant on a throne;
We see, some think, the greatest spot on earth,
For here each human being grows in worth.
We see a champion of true liberty,
Emancipator, Man of Destiny!
　　What inspiration ev'ry look imparts,
　　And we enshrine our hero in our hearts!

What do we hear while in this sacred place?
Just whispered plaudits by the human race?
Much more! Methinks I hear a trumpet blast,
A stirring, ringing challenge from the past.
This great incarnate conscience of our land,
Spoke in a voice all men could understand.
His warning words which rang with earnest tone,
Now echo through this monument of stone.
　　The price of liberty, he seems to say,
　　Is still eternal vigilance today!

What do we feel mid sculptured art so fine?
Just passing pride in this great national shrine?
Far more! We feel the heart throbs of our race,
While looking up at Lincoln's furrowed face.
A deep conviction stirs within our souls,
A burning zeal to reach our national goals.
We feel, while standing in this place sublime,
Inspired to grasp our heritage of time!
　　Thank God for Lincoln's call to great and small,
　　Of liberty and justice for us all!

On Seeking God

I sought God in each church in town;
  I climbed the highest steeple.
I heard God calling, "Son, come down;
  I'm with the lonely people."

And so I left my iv'ry tower
  To seek the brokenhearted.
Since then I've felt God's peace and power
  As I His love imparted.

Serenity With Discernment

Dear God, give us strength to accept with serenity the things
that cannot be changed. Give us courage to change the things that
can and should be changed. And give us wisdom to distinguish
one from the other.—REINHOLD NIEBUHR.

Dear God, give us the strength, we pray,
To face our lot in life each day,
Accepting things we cannot change,
With faith not fear, nor think it strange,
And not grow bitter, sour, or mean,
But meet these things and stay serene.

But there are other things, we know,
Which can and should be changed, and so,
We come to Thee and humbly ask
For courage to begin the task;
  But give us wisdom to see through
  The diff'rences between the two!

Teaching Like Jesus

If we would teach like Jesus taught,
　　What great results we'd see.
But no one speaks like Jesus spoke,
　　For no one lives as He.

He spent much time in study;
　　He spent much time in prayer.
For dealing with the human mind,
　　Each teacher must prepare.

Christ drew His lessons from the fields,
　　From mountains and the sea.
If we would teach like Jesus taught,
　　Use methods as did He!

Christ puts high value into life;
　　He puts rich meaning too,
And Christ puts holy purpose
　　Into everything we do.

Christ stirred imagination;
　　His lessons reached the heart.
Christ's teaching was a science.
　　It's still time's noblest art!

When will we catch this vision?
　　When will we take the time
To really teach as Jesus taught,
　　And do His work sublime?

Growth

My faith is growing,
  Knowing the Christ,
    Fuller and richer in *content.*
My joys are growing,
  Knowing the Christ,
    Deeper and wider in *extent.*
My love is growing,
  Knowing the Christ,
    Sweeter and purer in *intent.*

A Siren Song

The voice of riches sings a siren song,
  And lures unwary souls with strange appeal.
The grip of riches on man's heart is strong,
  And holds a miser's hands with bands of steel.

His wealth prevents the lowliness of mind,
  The childlike feelings in his heart have fled;
It smothers every thought of being kind,
  And even grudges children crusts of bread.

Man's wealth inspires a false sense of his strength;
  He feels secure with all his gold in banks.
Yet sometimes goes to almost any length,
  To get more wealth for which he gives no thanks.

Thus man is robbed of sweetest joys of earth;
  He's lost his sense of nothingness and need,
The things of truest value and of worth—
  For he was snared by siren songs of greed.

6

A Fuzzy Aim

When goals of life are worthy, and you set the mark up
  high,
Don't criticize the target when you're missing that bull's-
  eye.
The fault is not that target's, friend, the fault is yours, for
  shame,
And people must improve themselves if they'd improve their
  aim.

To shoot at any target is a really serious game;
May God protect the innocent when we've a fuzzy aim.
How many human casualties at hunting-season time;
The people killed each year by careless hunters is a crime.

Before you pull the trigger or you let the arrow fly,
You'd better double check the object blurred before your
  eye.
To know what you are aiming at eliminates mistakes,
The second look in life will save you many sad heartaches.

When teaching or when preaching—in fact, in all you do—
Be sure your thoughts are clear and always keep the end in
  view.
If you don't know your subject, then your answers will be
  lame,
For any fuzzy thinking means you'll have a fuzzy aim.

This type of fuzzy thinking is a plague we all should dread,
For one who shoots with fuzzy aim has surely lost his head.
So give most careful thought to what you do, for fun or
  fame;
Look well at life's objectives and don't shoot with fuzzy aim.

Love, the Greatest Thing in the World

A Poetic Commentary on 1 Corinthians 13

I may speak with tongues of angels above,
But I'm nothing but noise without God's love.
I might have the faith to do mighty deeds,
But my loveless life would show greater needs.
I may fill my mind with intellectual lore,
But I'm destitute if I've nothing more.
I might give my wealth with a lavish heart,
But God counts it naught if love plays no part.
I might give myself to a martyr's death,
But without real love, it's nothing but breath.

We need more than eloquence, wisdom, or wealth.
We must have real love to enjoy life and health.
Love is like fragrance from every crushed rose;
Love is the sweetest thing man or God knows.
Love is so patient, so thoughtful, so kind;
Love is the greatest thing you'll ever find.
Search it around the world, you'll search in vain.
You'll never find it by seeking your gain.
Love "seeketh not her own"; strongest in loss;
Love shines the brightest when seen on a cross.

Love is not touchy or selfish or rude,
Genuine love shows the right attitude.
Love is not happy when others go wrong;
Love helps the hopeless to sing a new song.
Love is not jealous, it makes no parade;
Love has good manners and gladly gives aid.
Love is so eager to believe what is best,

But seems so unwilling to expose the rest.
Hopeful and patient, true love never fails;
Above our poor preaching love ever prevails.
Now we know little; a new day will come
When we'll have true wisdom and not be so dumb.

When children grow up in their thinking, they cease
To argue like children; they then long for peace.

We're looking at life in mirrors, it seems,
And see but reflections of some of our dreams.
But when true reality bursts on our race,
We'll then see our Maker, at last, face to face.
We'll take a new look at Love, Faith, and Hope—
(No longer need tears as man's best telescope)—
We'll study God's truths in pure light from above,
And find that the greatest of God's gifts is Love!

Some Questions to Answer

Are our voices muted in these maudlin, muddled times?
Is our vision blinded by these bold and blatant crimes?
Is our witness weakened by an inconsistent life?
Have our swords been blunted, unprepared to face the
    strife?

Is my spirit sweeter? Am I kinder ev'ry day?
Have I lost my patience or my faith along the way?
Is my knowledge deeper? Are my gospel feet well shod?
Is my service richer when I wait to worship God?

When Loved Ones Pray

When loved ones pray for us, God draws so near;
How oft we've seen the dangers disappear!
One midnight when a great deliv'rance came,
My mother must have prayed for me by name.
She often wrote how she had ris'n at night
To pray for us who worked in hours of light
For those who lived the other side of earth.
I thank God for her prayers, their power and worth.*

When loved ones pray, the storm clouds disappear,
And we can see the star of hope shine clear,
Then courage comes—we feel a holy power,
The grace and strength to meet each trying hour.
Why do we dream of them; who comprehends?
Is it God urging us, *Plead for your friends?*
Oh, intercede for those so far away;
Help comes to meet their need when loved ones pray!

*It was Mother's custom to rise in the night to pray for us in
China where it was daylight and we would be working and would
need power from Heaven. But on this occasion I had been im-
prisoned for our faith, like Peter of old for whom the church
members were praying in the night when he was suddenly de-
livered by an angel (Acts 12:1-17). I too was strangely released from prison at midnight, so I was sure that Mother
had been praying in the daytime when we normally would be
sleeping. I cannot account for the strange surge of power I have
felt on many occasions except that Mother was praying for me.
"Prayer changes things!" God hears and answers prayer!

—THE AUTHOR

Criticism

To criticize another's sins cannot atone
For ours, or grant us right to cast the pointed stone.

"I'd Rather Keep My Song"

In the early years of the golden West
A pioneer preacher came with the rest.
The people loved him and they meant no harm
When they gave him a house and a lovely farm.

But later the pastor gave it all back
And he moved to a humbler, rented shack.
He said to his friends, "You have been so kind,
But I want to get back my peace of mind.

"For this was my song—'twas my choicest of themes—
As we crossed the prairies, mountains, and streams:
   'No foot of land do I possess,
   No cottage in this wilderness.'
Now you've spoilt my hymn, yet you meant no wrong,
But take the farm—I'd rather keep my song!"

Altitude or Attitude—Which?

We Christians long for higher heights;
   Up mountain peaks we plod.
What motivates desired delights?
   Why would we walk with God?

Do we desire to leave the plain
   Where sinful men abound
Because we're tired of toil and pain,
   And seek where peace is found?

Do we desire to rear our tent,
   Like Peter, on the hills?
A Christian, if he'd be content,
   Must share ecstatic thrills.

If we permit the men of earth
   To die beneath sin's rod,
Then our religion has no worth.
   How can we walk with God?

For God "so loved" the world of men,
   He sent Christ from on high;
And we must shout the news again,
   So no one needs to die.

The Master sends us down the mount
   Where sinners walk abroad,
To lead them to salvation's fount—
   This is to walk with God!

Who seeks for heights of solitude
   As heavenward he mounts,
Soon finds it isn't altitude
   But attitude that counts.

The Challenge of the Unknown

"Don't let the horizon be your boundary!"

There's a lure of the far horizon,
   Where the earth blends into the blue,
Where our faith displaces axioms
   With the challenge of something new!

It's as old as the trek of Abraham
   On his westward journey with God;
It's as new as your latest venture
   In the unknown paths you have trod.

It's the thing that inspired Columbus,
   And Marconi, Edison, Bell;
And it challenged the faith of Carey
   The darkness of earth to dispel.

There is treasure of rarest value
   At the rainbow's end, that is real,
For the greatest challenge that comes to man
   Is the lure of the Great Ideal!

Now the shortest distance between two points
   Is a straight line—a fact we know;
Yet *facts* don't stir us to do or die;
   It's *ideals* that cause us to grow!

For it's not the grasp of the facts we know
   That provides us life's greatest thrill;
It's the search for uncharted realities
   That will lure us beyond the hill!

O'er the rim of the world is your rainbow
   And the gold that is all your own,
For the glory of life with its challenge
   Is the lure of the Great Unknown!

Discoveries

"Without adventure, civilization is in full decay."

Within the mind of man there is, we're told,
A continent of undiscovered gold.
Vast treasures we may conquer or explore,
If we will launch our ships away from shore.

Above the Gates of Hercules some see
No more beyond—and with this they agree.
They will not risk a venture far abroad,
Like Abraham's great westward trek with God.

Or, like Columbus, cross an unknown sea
To find, beyond man's sight, what there might be.
Or like John Glenn, who took his leap in space
To add new luster to the human race.

He learned his lessons well; he knew his tools;
He *worked* his *faith* and he *obeyed the rules!*
He did not panic with the long delays,
But calmly rode the "fireball" through the haze.

He gave new meaning to the great word "GO"
And made it shine with iridescent glow.
How organized the timing and the crew;
And *"everything is go"* meant work to do!

The whole plan called for know-how and for brains;
Repeated practices and careful pains!
The only men who push horizons back
Believe the head is more than mere hatrack.

The world still needs such worthy pioneers
To clear the jungles of confused frontiers,
To pull each ugly thorn of hate that grows,
And make the desert blossom like the rose!
　　　　　—Written after Col. John H. Glenn
orbited the world three times, February 20, 1962.

Retention

Words without action are the assassins of idealism.—HERBERT
HOOVER.

It's not what we eat, how much or how long,
But what we digest that helps make us strong.

It's not what we study or read with our eyes,
But what we remember that helps make us wise.

It's not what we earn, while filling our niche,
But what a man saves that makes a man rich.

It's not what we preach, for words are low priced;
It's living His life that makes us like Christ.
　　　　　—4:15 A.M., *Tegucigalpa, Honduras*

Smiles Are Electrical

A sincere smile works magic any place;
　It warms and brightens with a matchless art,
For it's the lighting system of the face
　And it's the heating system of the heart!

Do You Love Life?

"He that will love life, and see good days, let him refrain his tongue from evil, and his lips that they speak no guile." 1 Peter 3:10.

> Do you love life?
>   From evil keep your tongue!
> If you love life,
>   'Twill help you to stay young.
>
> Do you love life?
>   Then never curse, but bless.
> If you love life,
>   Then share your happiness!

Avoid the Judgment Seat

Ezekiel sat "where they sat," and he sat there for a week
Before he had the courage or audacity to speak.
But some of us rush in, like fools, where angels fear to tread,
And with our own snap judgments make decisions we
    should dread.

Whene'er we fail to "double check the facts" we are unwise,
For jumping at conclusions is poor mental exercise.
May God protect the innocent when we've a fuzzy aim,
Because, as modern Pharisees, we have no sense of shame.

How different from the Master. When accusers grabbed a
    stone,
He wrote their sins upon the sand so each could see his
    own.
The Indians had a custom that was very good and wise:
Walk weeks in others' moccasins before you criticize!

The Better Way

We've heard about a Hyde Park Marxist, shouting while he
    brags,
  Of merits of his Communistic plan.
He pointed to a beggar who was drunk and dressed in rags,
  "We'll put a brand new suit upon that man."

An ardent, earnest Christian, who was standing by that day,
  Stepped forward as he joined in the dispute.
He calmly cried, "The Christian method is a better way;
  It puts a brand new man inside the suit!"

Full Sail Ahead

I've read about an old sailboat
    Whose sail was full of holes.
It crept along and kept afloat,
    But struggled toward its goals.

The old sailboat was always late;
    It never won a race.
The winds of God would dissipate
    Through each hole's empty space.

Just like that boat, some folks on earth
    Will never win life's race;
Their "negatives" will spoil their worth,
    Doomed by each vacant space.

Repair waste places in your mind,
    Then hoist a perfect soul;
You'll catch the winds of God and find
    You'll speed to reach life's goal!

Smile at the Weatherman

When God sends rain
Then don't complain.
Just learn to say
Each rainy day:
"I will rejoice,
For rain's my choice.

"Last year 'twas dry!
How we did sigh!
The sun was hot—
Have you forgot?
We prayed for rain;
Now don't complain."

Along the way,
From day to day,
A cheerful smile
Should spark each mile.
A smiling face
Helps win life's race!

I'm sure that he serves us the best that he can;
So let us all smile at the poor weatherman!

Little Lights

Good little children are so sweet,
  Their smiling faces seem divine,
They brighten paths for weary feet.
  They are God's little lights that shine;
  They lighten this dark world of mine.

Tribute to Dreamers

"Where there is no vision, the people perish." Prov. 29:18.
Where there is vision, the people do exploits.

Back of all life's achievements,
    Back of all goals that are reached;
Back of the toil and bereavements,
    Back of the great sermons preached;
Back of the fame and the glory
    Are teammates playing their part;
Back of each thrilling story
    Is love from a loyal heart.

Back of the deeds inspiring,
    Back of the plaudits and cheers,
Are those with brows perspiring,
    The men of vision, the seers,
The men who are called to be schemers,
    The thinkers, who plan what to do;
Back of success are the dreamers
    Who make their dreams come true!

The Eternal Quest

The lure and glory of the human mind
Is searching for the things which we may find
Beyond the border of the facts we know,
And in this search a man is bound to grow.

Remember Emerson's authentic voice
That God gives everyone on earth a choice
Between a search for truth or life of rest;
Man can't have both, in this eternal quest.

SECTION 5

In Merrier Mood

The Retort Beautiful

A visitor inquired with scornful eyes,
  "Can this town boast one single thing of worth?"
The native answered, "Sure! A man can rise
  And go from here to any place on earth!"
              —2:57 A.M., *Takoma Park, Maryland*

A Merry Mind

"A merry heart doeth good like a medicine." Prov. 17:22.
Unless you cultivate a cheerful, happy, grateful frame of mind,
Satan will eventually lead you captive at his will.—*Testimonies,*
vol. 1, p. 704.

The charming *curve* of a cheerful smile
Has power to *straighten* out problems that rile,
And keep you happier mile after mile.
 A smile's the style
 All the while.

Look up when you're down, and grin when "all in";
Despondency, sir, is a subtle sin.
The man who can smile is one who can win.
 To win just grin;
 The grin can win.

So brush away clouds and frowns from your face,
And brighten your life, your work, and your place
With smiles that inspire men to run life's race.
 The face with grace
 Sets life's true pace.

Such smiles must come from a heart that's kind;
When love is entwined, your work is no grind.
So, live all your life with a merry mind.
 The mind's the find
 For all mankind.

His Own Precious Promise

A little Chinese boy had searched the Bible for his name
(I'm sure that many other folks have likewise done the
 same).

How faithfully he studied, and ev'ry day he'd look
To try to find his name within the blessed Book.

And then one day he found it and his heart was filled with
    glee;
He rushed to show his pastor, who was pleased as he could
    be.
The little lad, whose name was Lo, then read these words so
    true:
"Lo, I am with you alway"! Does it make you happy, too?

On Snapping Fingers at What We Don't Like

I've heard about a man who snapped his fingers all the time,
And all his strange experiences just can't be put in rhyme.
But here is one we can relate. He told some men one day
Just why he snapped his fingers—"To keep lions far away."
His friends persuaded him to see a good psychiatrist.
The doctor watched him snap his fingers with that certain
    twist,
And asked him kindly *why* he snapped his fingers all the
    while;
And when he heard the reason, then he answered with a
    smile,
"Dear man, there's not a lion in a thousand miles from
    here!"
"So you see it is effective," snapped the patient with a leer.

Are we not just as stupid when we snap our fingers too,
At many things, or certain work we may not like to do?
Don't snap your fingers, friend, at death, or taxes, or at God,
Or at the work that must be done to spread the truth abroad!

Loving-kindness

A little boy was asked, one day, if he thought he could
    show
How loving-kindness differed from plain kindness; did he
    know?
He grinned and said, "I think I know why they are not the
    same.
When mother butters bread for me, that's kindness, so I
    claim;
But sometimes mamma is so sweet, she goes the second mile,
And heaps the nicest jam on top, and does it with a smile.
I have another name for that: it's LOVING-KINDNESS,
    sir,
And I am not ashamed to say, *it sure makes me love her!*"

A Riddle

All the wisdom of the ages,
All the knowledge of the sages,
You will find within the pages
    Of an old neglected book.

All the thoughts in English penned,
Which you'd like to comprehend,
You will find them all, my friend,
    In this old neglected book.*

Every thing that you can measure,
Every thought on work or pleasure,
Can you find this hidden treasure?
    Will you tell me where to look?

*Webster's New International Unabridged Dictionary.

The Home-run King

He struck out more than any man
  In all the hist'ry of the game,
And yet, if you're a baseball fan,
  You'll surely know his famous name.

He struck out thirteen hundred times,*
  But no one ever mentions that.
The people came from many climes
  To see him swing his mighty bat.

He gave the world a lesson grand:
  He would not quit or cease to swing.
That's why he's known in every land
  As great Babe Ruth—the home-run king.

* Babe Ruth struck out 1,330 times, a record in failure un-
matched by any other player in the history of baseball. But we
do not remember him for that. Disregarding his many failures, he
kept on trying and swinging, and finally closed his career with an
all-time record of 714 home runs. In the language of the sports
world, this man with 1,330 failures might have been called the
strike-out wonder, but the world knows him as the home-run king.

Fred's Version

A little boy had often heard folks say
Our Lord's sweet prayer in just the usual way;
But when, one day, he said it all alone,
He had a newer version all his own:
"Our Father, which art in heaven," he said,
"How'd you know my name?" then asked for bread.
I'm thankful for Fred's version just the same,
For I'm so glad that Jesus knows my name.

The World Looks Better From Behind a Smile

Do you know *why* some people fail?
Well, listen to this bookman's tale.
It seemed he was a hopeless case,
For he was such a sober kind,
He had a very serious mind,
And never wore a smile upon his face.

His leader counseled him awhile,
And told him that he ought to smile.
"The Bible says, 'Be sober,'" he declared.
So he went on, but doomed to fail.
At last he came with his sad tale,
And said, "I want to quit; I have despaired."

The leader counseled him again,
Explained to him why meeting men
Requires that we must smile, that "smiling pays."
"Before you quit, try out this plan,
And learn to be a smiling man."
He said, "All right, I'll try to mend my ways."

So he went back and really smiled;
The people seemed to be beguiled,
They bought his books and he had lots of fun.
The first four homes he sold four books.
He found it matters how one looks,
And smiling helps to get the good work done.

He wrested vict'ry from defeat;
The spoils of triumph were so sweet,
He said he'd never had such joy before.
And when that glorious week was past
He counted up his gains at last,
But told his boss, "You know, my face is sore!"

The Danger of Indifference

We never dare stop in our drive to the top,
  Or relax in a rut, satisfied.
For any such man there is only one plan—
  Make his grave in his rut where he died.

A story is told of a frog who grew cold
  In a rut in an old wagon road.
It seemed like the end, and he told ev'ry friend
  That he couldn't get out with his load.

The very next day he was seen on his way,
  And more chipper by far than before.
'Twas then his friends said, "We thought you were dead,
  And we'd see you around no more."

He said with a grin, "I'll let you all in
  On the secret, the *how* and the *why!*
As I sang my sad song, a truck came along,
  And I had to leap out or I'd die!"

Prescription for Health

  A simple diet with a merry mind,
  Two helpful hands, a tongue that's always kind;
  Deep breathing of pure air—still free from tax;
  While eating meals and after work, *relax!*

  Two smiling eyes to prove you still can laugh;
  Live simpler lives and cut your bills in half.
  A task you love, a conscience crystal clear;
  A heart at rest, a mind that's free from fear.

Use water freely, more within, without;
Have faith in God and give no place to doubt.
Then exercise your body, mind, and soul;
Look up and keep your eyes upon life's goal.

"Sitting on Top of the World"

A New York newspaper reported this tale:
A "drunk" kept on singing while taken to jail:
"I'm sitting on top of the world" was his song—
'Twas far from convincing, for he was dead wrong.
He was not on top of the world, as he said;
The world was on him from his feet to his head.
Deceived by King Alcohol, he was a mess,
As all those who saw him would have to confess.
Oh, why will a man of sense go to the pains
To pour in his mouth what will plunder his brains?

A man is on top when he's in full control
Of all of the vices that war with his soul;
On top of the forces that drag a man down—
His appetites, hatreds, or even his frown.
On top of anxiety, doubt disappears;
On top of his greed and on top of his fears;
On top of his temper, on top of his tongue,
On top of his passions to which he had clung.
On top of his selfishness, even his pride,
When faith and true love in a great rising tide
Keep flooding his life, and he cries out for more;
He's filled with such joy that his heart bubbles o'er.
His "body kept under," as Paul used to say,
He knows of a Saviour for each castaway.

On top of his work and on top of the heap
Of details of life that make other men weep.

On top of his worries, with Christ in control,
He conquers the forces that war with his soul.
He shouts, "To the family of God I belong!"
"I'm sitting on top of the world!" is *his* song!
—4:45 A.M., *Berrien Springs, Michigan*

Crime Does Not Pay

As oft we see, variety
   Is still life's rarest spice;
It breaks the drab monotony
   If we can pay the price.

This tale we know, may seem to show
   The seamy side of life.
But it will show, despite its woe,
   With humor life is rife.

A cat had died, the owner cried
   Because she loved her pet.
But she was brave, she'd dig a grave—
   A grave she'd not forget.

So, orthodox, a nice shoe box
   Would be the resting place.
Since she was kind, a spot she'd find
   And bury it with grace.

But on her way, that very day,
  She stopped at one big store,
And left the box (with car unlocked)
  Inside the back seat door.

When she came out, she gave a shout,
  Her precious box was gone.
But why weep more—she'd shop till four,
  And then go home anon.

Inside the store, she walked the floor,
  Then passed a large rest room.
She stepped inside, and—petrified—
  She saw a sight of doom.

Inside the door, sprawled on the floor
  A fainted woman lay.
And close beside, box opened wide,
  Her dead cat on display.

She took her cat, and after that,
  She calmly walked away,
And out of town, a spot she found
  And placed her cat that day.

I wish I knew, what did *she* do,
  When *"thief"* came to that day?
The cat was gone, would she go on,
  Or say, "Crime does not pay"?

Modern Rip van Winkle

We find in folklore more than oft appears,
Like Rip van Winkle's sleep of twenty years;
We're not surprised that he could sleep so long,
For many people do that right along!

But three strange things I cannot understand—
He slept while revolution swept the land!
He went so long, neglecting daily bread,
He passed into a coma, like one dead!

He slept indifferent to the changing world;
With nations born, new flags were then unfurled.
The picture of George Washington soon hung
Where George the Third's had been when Rip was young.

But he had missed the glory of it all,
For he had failed to heed his country's call.
He slept, impervious to the tragic need,
And, like a man in coma, took no heed.

What lessons we may learn from such a tale,
We find some reasons why so many fail.
Who starves his soul, refusing food to eat,
Soon drugs himself with his own self-conceit.

Thus stupefied he sees no crisis hour;
Thus hypnotized he feels no need of power;
And so he sleeps away his days of grace—
No sleeper renders service to his race.

And now we face the greatest hour of all,
But some, in coma, cannot hear God's call.
While sleeping, they are missing all the fun—
They'll miss the glory when God's work is done.

Recharging Life's Storage Battery of Curiosity

"Choose now your rut; You'll be there 20 miles"
This old Canadian road sign brings forth smiles.
Alas! Life's greater blunder, it appears,
Is being in a rut for twenty years!

Without adventure, life will soon decay.
What is man's greatest loss when he grows gray?
"When we are old we cease to play," we're told.
But no! We cease to play, *Then* we grow old!

Each child receives a boon when he is born,
A precious gift on that eventful morn—
A mind that can inquire; life's golden key,
A built-in box of curiosity!

We search through life for truth and what is right,
And ev'ry morning brings us fresh insight.
As we proceed along our rugged way,
Let's keep our storage battery charged each day!

We're young as long as we have hopeful eyes;
But we are old the day our courage dies!

Music Is Medicine

The use of music through the hours
    By those who practice healing arts
Reveals its therapeutic powers
    Recorded on the patients' charts.

For music now is used, you see,
    To wake us or bring slumbers.
The pieces played in surgery,
    Of course, are "opening numbers."

SECTION 6

Seasonal Verse

The Vision of the New Year

An angel comes and knocks once more,
And opens up the New Year door;
Unveils a vision sharp and clear
Of greater deeds this great New Year;
Then urges us to RISE and GO
And tell the world the good we know.
The angel leaves, but not in vain,
The blessed vision will remain!

Happy New Year

You must not dread the year ahead,
For what can fear and worry do
But steal away your strength today
And leave a poorer, weaker you?

So greet the year with hope and cheer,
For worry never rights a wrong.
Resolve, my dear, to persevere,
And sing a Happy New Year song!

Another Chance

Another year, another chance
To take new courage and advance
To better things that lie ahead,
And profit by the past, now dead.

It is indeed another chance
To take a hasty backward glance
And see what caused mistakes I've made,
Then face the future unafraid.

Another year, another chance
To master ev'ry circumstance.
The fires of love I must renew,
And purify all things untrue.

Another year, another chance
To do my utmost to enhance
Man's faith in God and spread good cheer—
That I resolve to do this year!

Kneel With the Wise Men

Before the Babe of Bethlehem we kneel,
With shepherds and the Wise Men, and we feel
The ecstasy that humble worship brings,
Which stirs the hearts of shepherds or of kings.

We learn such precious lessons as we meet
And wait in willing worship at His feet.
We kneel with kings, we kneel with shepherds too.
There is no caste from Heaven's point of view.

There is a place for rich and for the poor;
There is a place for babies, that is sure;
There is a place for women. God is good
To glorify the worth of womanhood.

There's something noble in each child of God.
Arise! Let's spread this glorious news abroad.

Season's Greetings

As Old Year ends,
   With New Year just ahead,
We'd greet our friends
   And hearty good cheer spread.
We face our task—
   God's work—that must be done
E'er we can bask
   Beneath heav'n's peaceful sun.
We join and pray,
   As New Year looms in view,
May God convey
   His best on all of you!

A Happier New Year

'Tis time for New Year bells to ring
The year's first harbinger of spring.
Our eager hands now grasp the rope
To ring sweet bells of peace and hope.

Ring out the Old Year's sin and strife;
Ring in the more abundant life.
Since EVIL is just LIVE spelled wrong,
Why not LIVE right and make life strong?

Why backward LIVE and EVIL do?
This year let God make *all* things new!
Our New Year greetings now we bring,
And happier New Year bells we'd ring!

P.S. (*Poetic Script*):

LIVE spelled backward is EVIL! True!
Thus LIVED we have the DEVIL, too!
Let's take "I" out of LIVE this year,
And let the LOVE of Christ appear.
When "I" am "O" (nothing) there's no loss—
True LOVE will glorify a cross!

My Garden

My garden is a place of cheer,
With fragrant flowers blooming here;
And lovely birds delight to sing—
Especially when it is spring.

Peace on Earth

"Peace on earth, good will to men"—
Let's sing the rapturous song again!
Around our world so much that's wrong
Would cease, if men could hear this song!

But songs alone won't do the work
If only sung within the kirk.
Let's sing it, *live it,* in the home;
Let's sing it everywhere we roam.

Let's hum it at our work or play;
Let's seek it when we kneel to pray.
Let's practice it in shop or store;
Let's take it to our neighbor's door.

Let's live it while we're on the train;
Let's carry it up in the plane.
Let's sing it in the bus or car;
Let's talk of peace instead of war.

Let's shout it everywhere we go,
And preach it so all men will know
The magic touch, transforming power
Of Christ, the need of this great hour!

So as the New Year comes again,
Share "peace on earth, good will to men."
Let's catch the cadence of the theme,
And help fulfill man's fondest dream.

Let's spread above earth's blood-soaked sod
This wondrous peace and love of God!

A Prayer for the New Year

"Daniel purposed *in his heart."* Dan. 1:8.

God, give us power to live out what we know;
    Make us sincere as we attempt to teach.
Make us consistent as the truth we show;
    God, grant us grace to practice what we preach!

Words without works will kill as with a spear
    Our better selves, and ev'ry high ideal.
God, help us stretch our dreams to deeds this year,
    With rock-ribbed *purpose* and *with wills of steel.*

O God, our time on earth with speed is spent,
    So make us conscious of our deepest need:
The will to build upon each good intent,
    And make each noble thought a noble deed!

When Christmas Comes

When Christmas comes we join and sing
Sweet carols to our Lord and King.
But Christmas means much more than song,
For other things somehow belong.
It is the season of the year
When we desire to share our cheer;
Our messages, or gifts, we send
To loved ones or time-honored friend.
Our sentiments we then renew,
And letters write—long overdue—
To mother who each day did wait
Beside the mailbox near the gate.

With hopeful steps she walked that trail
And grasped the mailbox for her mail.
She pulled the tight-lipped door apart
And found it—empty, like her heart!
How often she has come in vain
And felt that piercing, poignant pain
Of loneliness a mother feels,
And unrequited love conceals.

Then Christmas comes; at last we write.
The mailbox dances with delight.
And mother smiles through tears of joy—
At last she's heard from her "dear boy."
How wonderful one day can heal
The pain a lonely heart may feel.
When Christmas comes our gifts we give
And many folks learn how to live.
Behold the power that Christmas packs
When even misers' hands relax!
We all are led somehow to share
Our joy with humans everywhere.
We sing the same sweet songs again
Of peace on earth, good will to men.

When Christmas comes we sense release
From selfishness, and we find peace.
What miracles are in the air,
What transformations everywhere!
O God, what changes we survey!
What happiness has come our way!
If one day can so much convey,
Why not have Christmas every day?

8

When Christ Is in Christmas

When Christ is in Christmas
   There's bound to be love
For that's why He came from
   His heaven above.

When Christ is in Christmas
   There's bound to be peace;
All bitterness, hatred,
   And worry will cease.

When Christ is in Christmas
   There's bound to be joy,
For He was God's gift of
   A sweet baby boy.

When Christ is in Christmas
   There's bound to be power,
A magical something that
   Transforms each hour!

Is Christ in *your* Christmas?
   Then merry's the day.
You've found, like the Wise Men
   A far better way!

"No Vacancy"

'Twas while the world lay gripped with fear
   And crushed beneath the Roman heel
That angels sang their songs of cheer
   And shepherds heard their sweet appeal.

In spite of war, they sang of peace,
  The dawning of a better day.
Though wealth of cities would increase,
  Man's moral life would soon decay.

Observe the state of man that morn,
  The busy cities' piteous plight.
The only place Christ could be born
  Was in a humble barn that night.

But should the Christ return tonight,
  Where could He find a place to stay?
Would Inns announce with neon light,
  "NO ROOM"? Is No what we still say?

Beauty of the Springtime

*"Dead flies cause the ointment of the apothecary to send forth
a stinking savour."*—Eccl. 10:1.

It's really great to be alive
  When beauty of the springtime comes;
Along the flow'r-lined roads we drive,
  And tune our harps to nature's drums.
    But while our souls burst forth in song,
    Can *that* drown *this* world's wail of wrong?
      Let's not forget, when springtime comes,
      The bitter ballads of the slums!

It's wonderful how spring flow'rs bloom
  To bless and brighten all our ways;
And as we breathe their sweet perfume,
  Our hearts respond in grateful praise.

But while we pause in thankful prayer
For all this fragrance in the air,
Let's not forget, when springtime comes,
The stench that rises from the slums!

How wonderful if we, this spring,
  Would take fresh flowers to each dark door;
I think that it might help us sing
  Some songs we never sang before.
    As we our hope and perfume share,
    How many might join us in prayer!
      So let's resolve, as this spring comes,
      To carry springtime to the slums!
                    —3:30 A.M., *Tokyo, Japan*

April in the Soul

We must not be content with what we are;
Remember: "Hitch your wagon to a star!"
In this space age that still is good advice,
If we would reach our home in Paradise.
Resurging spring revives man's fading goal;
Each person needs an April in his soul!

Spring Is Here

I sensed a stirring in the trees
And thought at first it was the breeze,
But when I turned and looked again
I felt the power of sun and rain.

Within the span of these few weeks
I've heard the message nature speaks;
Pulsating power crept through the earth,
And all of nature had rebirth.

I saw life leaping from the sod—
The resurrection power of God!
Without fanfare or roll of drum,
I realized that spring had come!

Kind Echoes

Speak kind words of hope and cheer,
Kind echoes you will always hear.

My Sixtieth Birthday Prayer

Dear God, today I pass a new milestone;
I celebrate a day that's all my own.
I've lived for sixty years before Thine eyes,
And ev'ry day has brought some fresh surprise.
It's wonderful how sweet a life can be
When walking all the way, O Lord, with Thee.
With deepest gratitude I come to pray,
And thank Thee that I've lived to see this day.
As I review these sixty wondrous years,
I see how oft Thy guiding hand appears.
I thank Thee for my mother's tender care,
And for her patient love and daily prayer.
I thank Thee too that early in my youth
I learned to know and love Thy precious truth.

And I was just a lad still in my teens
When Thou didst call me hence to distant scenes.
Around the world we've worked for forty years,
And walked together through earth's vale of tears.
I'm thankful too that early in my life
At our own school I met my future wife.
I'm thankful for our children born abroad,
While we were in the service of our God.
I thank Thee for the things I've seen and heard;
I praise Thee for the treasures of Thy Word.
As visions of the future come in view
I thank Thee for the great work we must do.
I celebrate this day this side the sea—
And dedicate my life anew to Thee!
                    —4:45 A.M., *Bandung, Java*

Welding Past and Present for a Greater Future

As now we pause inside this New Year's gate,
It is a fitting time to meditate;
To take a rear-view mirror look behind,
And see what gains or losses we may find;
The failures of the past we must forget—
Save only fire, not ashes of regret!

Let's make TODAY our transmutation time,
Then YESTERDAY can help to make sublime
TOMORROW'S records—greater than the past,
And through the Christ, a finished work at last;
Let's WELD THE PAST to this DYNAMIC HOUR,
And see the FUTURE outbursts of God's power!

SECTION 7

Sunset and Evening Bell

Life's Little Day

This morn my newborn babe, with childish charm,
   Slipped from my lap and toddled off to school.
She came back leaning on a young man's arm;
   Their son brings grandma's shawl as night grows cool.

The Secret of Contentment

"With books the poorest man is rich;
Without books the richest man is poor."

Before I learned the secret of contentment,
  I viewed my lot in life with ill-concealed contempt,
And in my bitter heart I felt resentment
  Against the place, the men, each task I would attempt.

And then I found the secret of contentment;
  I saw by reading books a way to change my mind;
And it became my life's supreme investment,
  For through one precious Book I learned to love mankind.

Now when I open books, new windows open wide,
  And when I open books, doors seem to swing ajar.
I visit with the good, and with the great I ride,
  And make adventures in my books to realms afar.

Since I have found the treasures of contentment,
  I love the people and I like my work and place.
No longer do I feel the least resentment—
  I have my books and dreams, which transcend time and
    space!

                              —3:55 A.M., *Detroit, Michigan*

Growing Old Gracefully

Dear God, while I am growing old,
Please keep my heart from growing cold.
Though years may wrinkle up my skin,
And even wrinkle up my grin,
May nothing wrinkle up my soul
Or rob me of my self-control.

Give me the warmth of love and grace
To keep a smile upon my face.
In spite of all my aches and pain
Please help me never to complain.
And may I never look cast down,
Or at the little children frown.
I want no child to run from me,
As from a shrunken, haunted tree.
So may I radiate such cheer
That all their fear will disappear.

As I grow old teach me the art
And secret of the happy heart!

Stay Young!

Since only the body of man grows old,
The soul will stay young, if we wish, we're told.

We're young as our faith, as old as our doubt;
We're young as our smile, as old as our pout.
We're old as our hate, as old as our fears;
We cease to be young when love disappears.
Why should we grow bitter or sad or sour,
When only a smile could sweeten each hour?

The longer the fruit can grow on a tree,
The sweeter and better that fruit will be!
So we should be sweeter the longer we live—
Grow *better,* not bitter, and learn to forgive!
Be sure that you speak only kind words each day,
Then you'll hear kind echoes while you're growing gray.

You're young as the smile from your hopeful eyes;
You're old on the day when your courage dies.
So keep your lamps burning at eventide—
The close of life's day should be glorified!
Life's sunset can glow through your eyes and your
    tongue—
With Faith and with radiant Love—STAY YOUNG!

Time

The time of life is short; to spend that shortness basely were too long.—SHAKESPEARE.

"Time slips away,"
We sometimes say.
Is that the truth we should convey?
Time stays; life goes,
Like fragrant rose,
That blooms in beauty for a day.

Life is too brief
For hate or grief.
Life is so sweet my glad heart sings.
Life is sublime!
Can we find time—
With life so great—for petty things?

Destined for Glory

Onward Christian laymen, marching in your might,
Going forth with Jesus, forward with the light.
You will tell His story, filled with Heaven's power,
Destined soon for glory, matched for time's last hour.

God Speaks the Last Word

Though skeptics shout until they're hoarse,
The stars still keep their ordered course,
And silently reveal God's force.

The fool may say, "There is no God!"
And yet God sheds His love abroad,
And feeds the fool from fruitful sod.

Yet puny man still shuts his eyes
To all the glory of the skies.
God speaks the last word when man dies!

Maturity

The years can teach us many things
    Which moments never know;
The rosebud opens to the one
    Who calmly lets it grow.

Don't pluck the peach from off the tree
    While still the fruit is green;
Permit the sunshine and the rain
    To add a golden sheen.

Maturity is God's sweet gift
    To bless the human race;
In patience wait for God to make
    More than a pretty face.

For character is needed too,
    To meet earth's stress and strife,
And one must train in arts and skills
    To have a happy life.

Where Was God?

I lost my dad when I was just a boy,
  But I was then too young to question God.
Another loved one, my own pride and joy,
  Quite recently I buried 'neath the sod.

For over forty years it's been my task,
  As minister, to lay away the dead.
I've stood by countless loved ones as they ask,
  "Why should we have to face this fearful dread?"

"Why should my loved one have to lifeless lie?"
  "Why should this sad experience come to me?"
"Where was God when my dear boy had to die?"
  I answer: "Where He was when His Son died
    for thee!"

No More Death

We oft have stood beside the open grave;
  We've seen our loved ones going one by one;
We think we know just how we should behave
  When death arrives and one more life is done.

But facing death is not an easy task;
  Our hearts are pierced with pain for ev'ry friend.
Beside each grave we cannot help but ask,
  "When will this tragic sorrow have an end?"

In silence comes the sweetest voice I've heard,
  With hope for hearts that sorrow has made sore,
"Recall My promises; I'll keep My word;
  Within My kingdom death shall be no more."

Whence Cometh Consolation?

Whence cometh consolation when our souls are sorely tried,
While looking on the faces of our loved ones who have died?
And there are other tragedies and troubles worse than death,
And accidents so shocking you can hardly catch your breath.

Whence cometh consolation when, with body pierced with
      pains,
We face financial losses which have wiped out lifetime
      gains?
Then, after all these troubles that make mind and body ache,
There comes some crushing news to try and make the strong
      heart break!

Whence came Job's consolation when the cyclone came his
      way?
He lost his wealth, his property, and children in a day.
Then when his health and strength were gone, his wife and
      friends gave up,
And all alone he had to drink life's bitter, trembling cup.

Job could not lift the curtain up and look behind the veil,
So did not know the reason, but his faith—it did not fail!

"Sweet Be Thy Sleep"

How precious is the peaceful sleep
    Of ev'ry one God calls a saint.
Is death a time for us to weep,
    And fill God's ears with our complaint?

Is death fulfillment of a dream,
    And from earth's shrouded, shrinking shore,
We launch upon an unknown stream?
    No! Death is sleep! Dare man say more?

The sleep of working men is "sweet,"
    So wrote the wisest man of all;
When our life's labors are complete,
    Thus be our "sleep" till God shall call.

Yes, death provides a time to rest
    Through all the storms of earth's dark night,
Until the saints who've stood life's test
    Will hear God's call to realms of light.

That resurrection morn will come
    When sleeping saints will hear God's voice,
And hail the blest millennium,
    And God and man will then rejoice!

If death is "precious" in His sight,
    As each dear saint is laid to rest,
Why should we doubt? God must be right,
    And what is right must be the best.

When Jesus comes the graves will ope,
    The saints will rise to see Christ come.
This is indeed *"the blessed hope,"*
    The hope of all of Christendom!

"Like as a Father"

We often face sorrows or suff'ring or grief,
And sometimes, like Job, get no human relief.
'Tis then, if we search, we may find in the Book
A picture of God that we can't overlook.

Christ taught us to call Him Our Father above—
Our Father—with infinite, measureless love.
He showed His disciples that wonderful day
That Father was near, only one prayer away.

Christ says, "I am with you," His peace to impart.
He feels ev'ry pain that you feel in your heart.
He asks you to trust, though your vision be dim,
And whispers, "Cast *all* of your care upon Him."

"He careth for you!" 'Tis a promise so sweet,
I stand overwhelmed, and I fall at His feet
To ask Him for mercy to stand ev'ry test
And faith that "all things" will work out for the best!

What comfort to know that whatever betide,
Lo, *"Like as a father,"* God stands by my side!
                    —5:00 A.M., *Karlsruhe, Germany*

A Tribute to Music

Good music builds a bridge with sound or song
    O'er which man's fettered feet may calmly climb
From earth's discordant prison house of wrong
    To realms of rhythm and symmetry sublime;
And by the means of music he grows strong,
    And sings of sweet release with rapturous rhyme.
Thus we, on wings of music, take our flight
From dungeon of death to worlds of light,
And find our freedom from earth's noisy night.
Is harmony high heaven's healing art?
Is it the worship of the human heart?

Possessing charm that soothes the savage breast,
Its melody can bring the weary rest.
Such is the power, in "concord of sweet sound,"
Among the greatest forces man has found.

The Afterglow

Why this mad race for place and pomp and power?
Why all this toil for triumphs of an hour?
What though we wade in wealth or worldly fame,
Can these endure time's fierce and final flame?

However great the man, at last he dies;
Earth's highest tribute ends in "Here he lies."
The richest man cannot his days prolong,
And "dust to dust" concludes life's sweetest song.

Ere our heart's blazing hearth shall cease to burn,
Time's winnowed wisdom we must somehow learn:
At death, what we have done for self alone
Will die with us; so, this grand truth enthrone:

What we have done for others will live on
To bless our mem'ry after we are gone!
Our unsung deeds the world *now* may not know,
Yet comes at last the radiant afterglow!